A Camera at the Ballet

Books by the same author

A Camera at the Ballet

Pioneer Dancers of the Royal Ballet

Gordon Anthony

DAVID & CHARLES

Newton Abbot   London   Vancouver

Dedication
For my grand-children Ruth and Louise James with my love.
Acknowledgments
John Duguide. For suggesting and bullying me into writing the articles. John Nash and Antony Latham of The Victoria and Albert Museum to whom I am exceedingly grateful for all their kind co-operation, and above all for permission to reproduce my pictures from their archives.

0 7153 6717 X

Set in 11 on 13 Imprint and printed in
Great Britain by Compton Printers, Aylesbury
for David & Charles (Holdings) Limited
South Devon House, Newton Abbot, Devon

Published in Canada by Douglas David & Charles Limited
3645 McKechnie Drive, West Vancouver BC

Contents

Introduction

It gives me a very special pleasure to write an introduction to this book by Gordon Anthony. When, at the age of about fifteen, I discovered my way to Sadler's Wells Theatre and its ballet company – travelling there from South London on a tram through the old Kingsway Tunnel – my most treasured possession was Gordon Anthony's book, *The Vic-Wells Ballet*. It was the first ballet book I ever owned; a collection of portraits and studio pictures of the dancers I worshipped.

By then, of course, Gordon Anthony was a very great and famous international photographer. His superb albums on *Russian Ballet* and *Massine* caught all the glamour of those Ballet Russe companies who bridged the gap and held a ballet audience from the death of Diaghilev in 1929 until the emergence of national companies in Great Britain and the United States. He photographed all the dancers and the ballets of the 1930s and his pages of pictures in *The Bystander* were, by me, villainously stolen from hairdressers and from dentists' waiting rooms. His contribution at that time to public appreciation of ballet can not be over-stressed; I stole the pages, but a huge readership bought the magazine, looked at the photographs and was influenced by them.

Very many years later I found myself, as editor of *The Dancing Times*, in a position to publish a series of articles by Gordon Anthony on the pioneers of the Royal Ballet. A chance remark by a child at the Royal Ballet School made me realise that the contributions to the building of our Royal Ballet by the artists pictured within are hardly known to young dancers of today. The child came across a picture of one of these pioneers – now her teacher – and said 'Goodness, were *you* once a dancer?' Something had to be done. We ran the series and it was enormously popular. Those who remembered the dancers were enchanted, nostalgic for the artists they had admired when they too were young. The students were fascinated to learn how people they knew as teachers or mime artists had paved the way for the great company that is the Royal Ballet of today.

I hope this book can appeal to all ages. It is, in one sense, a period piece; it is also a part of ballet history.

MARY CLARKE

Prologue

Miss Lillian Bayliss 1934. 'The Lady', Pioneer of English Opera Shakespeare and Ballet. Deeply religious, shrewd, forthright and indefatigable.

Perhaps I should explain for the sake of those new to the world of ballet that The Royal Ballet Company was born in 1929 at the Old Vic theatre which specialised in Opera and Shakespeare. Known as the Old Vic dancers, they were a small group headed by Ninette de Valois and pupils from her school. They appeared under the auspices of that intrepid, loved, honoured, and very much obeyed woman Lilian Baylis, affectionately known as 'The Lady'. They were greatly helped by the generosity of such guest artists as Lydia Lopokova, Stanislas Idzikowski, Ruth French, Anton Dolin, Phyllis Bedells and Alicia Markova, who later became a member of the company. Also to those many artists who were non permanent members of the

Ninette de Valois 1926. 'Madame'. Pioneer of two National Ballets. A dedicated, practical, intellectual, mercurial, idealist.

company which included Stanley Judson, Hermione Darnborough, Walter Gore, Hedley Briggs, Frank Staff, Anthony Tudor and Travis Kemp.

Although 'The Lady' took on the young Miss de Valois, she had no real faith in the project; so I now quote extracts from a foreword written by her for a book of Kate Neatby's on 'Ninette de Valois and The Vic-Wells Ballet' in 1934: – 'Ninette bided her time . . . she persuaded me to give one whole evening once a fortnight to ballet performances, frankly I confess I did not believe these could be anything but an artistic success . . . I was wrong . . . it was ballet to a tremendous extent that put Sadler's Wells on the map . . . I believe British ballet today has a better chance of survival than it has throughout the ages.' She was right!

I remember one evening when the Wells was packed to bursting point meeting Miss Baylis in the foyer, and the following conversation: 'Good evening Miss Baylis and congratulations on a marvellous house . . . oh well dear, it's all *so* expensive.' With which remark she promptly shot off and demanded the audience to do and *give* more for her dear 'boys and girls'. And they did!

Miss Baylis was a great builder and de Valois a great architect. It is no wonder that between them they laid the foundations of a terpsichorian mansion of such wondering and lasting beauty as The Royal Ballet. It was during that period the company became known as The Vic-Wells Ballet, from which it grew into The Sadler's Wells Ballet which, after the granting of the Royal charter in 1956 became the Royal Ballet of today, whose stars, starlets, soloists, and artists of the ballet (corps de ballet) are known from here to Timbuctoo.

But what of the stars of the 1930s? To my mind the favourites of the 30s become pioneers in the 70s, nearly half a century later. It seems quite shocking to think that many of them are forgotten, or not even heard of, by a great many ballet goers of today. A few of those dancers are still with the organisation as guest artists, ballet masters and mistresses, repetiteurs and teachers, amongst whom are Pamela May, Michael Somes, Julia Farron, Leslie Edwards and many others who were too young to be anything but choryphées and soloists in those exciting pioneering days.

1 Ninette de Valois

Ninette de Valois in Les Rendezvous. *'The lovers' pas de trois of witty nonsense arranged for her with Walter Gore and Stanley Judson. Ashton couldn't have given her anything more suitable for her type of dancing.*

DAME NINETTE DE VALOIS is my sister and to write about her is extremely difficult, and dangerous! In fact our relationship has no bearing whatever upon my thoughts and appreciation of her public life about which so much has already been written, including her own two books *Invitation to the Ballet,* 1935, and *Come Dance with Me,* 1956. So one can only write a little, a lot, or not at all—which is understandably her preference.

10

Those who know de Valois well are fully aware of her almost pathological dislike of personal publicity. Most famous ballet companies have been and still are known under the names of their founders—Diaghilev, de Basil, Massine, Rambert, Jooss, etc.—but her outlook was purely nationalistic, based upon long-term survival. Her company has chronologically been named The Vic-Wells, The Sadlers Wells and finally The Royal Ballet. The captain retired in 1963 and the old ship sails on. In actual fact she is the architect of two National ballets, for she founded the Turkish National Ballet over twenty years ago and still directs it. Before continuing on general lines I must quote a most interesting and amusing description of her as a child about 1909, and later on in the 'thirties, written by a one-time very lovely child dancer called June Trip, now a Mrs. Hillman.

'. . . led by a starched nurse, in so many frills and furbelows the poor child could hardly move . . . full of airs and graces.' In 1930 they meet again. ' . . . no trace of the pretty affected child in the intense young woman with smooth dark hair drawn austerely back from her oval face. Fame wears a variety of cloaks, Ninette's is simple, unglittering and becoming her to perfection.' I think this is the best description I have seen or heard of her. I always think of Ninette as a cross between Florence Nightingale and Good Queen Bess, particularly the latter, rolling heads in the dust one moment in a flaming rage and in the next roaring with laughter at some absurdity, blasting her ministers to a Protestant hell in one room, rushing madly off to dance the Bishop of Chester's jig in another! Elizabeth I kept everyone guessing; kept her policies to herself, her bark often worse than her bite, and to quote her chief minister, Sir William Cecil, 'when her counsellors said all they could suggest she would frame out a wise council beyond all theirs'. De Valois has all Elizabeth's sagacity, judgment and foresight minus her avarice, vanity and love of personal aggrandisement. She has the practical constructive tenacity of purpose, simplicity of living, understanding and toughness of the redoubtable Florence Nightingale. Both women were pioneers with a lack of physical strength overcome by their tenacity and fantastic nervous energy. Nightingale put the nursing profession on its feet; de Valois established the international reputation of British ballet.

As a dancer Ninette had a sound technique, and in her youth a brilliant one, well deserving of her title as one of Britain's leading *première danseuses*. Her dancing was mentioned as far back as 1910 in a book by Mark Perugini, and more fully in Ethel Urlin's book *Dancers Ancient and Modern,* in 1914.

'. . . a charming child genius glowing to her fingertips with the enthusiasm of the artist with her own interpretations of Chopin and Rubenstein waltzes, leaves a memory which is ideal in its combination of child-like innocence with artistic perfection of form. . . .'

In her work during the Vic-Wells and Sadlers Wells days she showed a gorgeous sense of humour and finesse; she was also one of the best pizzicato dancers of her day. In *Coppelia* she was a delightfully gay, bossy Swanilda, demonstrating her natural leadership in the treatment of her friends. She only danced the first two acts, but her interpretation of the Scottish and Spanish dances was of a phenomenal speed and precision of footwork with an almost 'saucy' gaiety. In her own ballets of *Douanes* and *Barabau,* her sense of style, timing and pastiche, were shown to great advantage. She possessed a charming Gaelic elegance and her portrait of the girl with the bottle in *Barabau* was incredibly funny, heightened by a mad sort of dignity. Her's was the secret of doing the minimum and looking the maximum. Ninette had developed into a demi-character dancer who would have been an ideal Bluebird with her swift birdlike head, arm, and leg movements, so totally unsuited as they were in *Les Sylphides* and *Spectre de la Rose.* Anything slow—and sentimentality—was completely foreign to her character.

Choreographically de Valois has three works to her credit of international fame, namely, *Job, The Rake's Progress,* and *Checkmate.* It was her choreography which first made me think of her as an architect, for every step, character, piece of music and human drama seemed carefully calculated and mathematically built up to a remarkably effective climax, particularly noticeable in *Checkmate.* It was some of her earliest works which gave one the impression of a great future for her in this field, especially *Creation du Monde,* 1933, and later *Prometheus,* 1936, followed by *Orpheus and Eurydice,* 1941. In this ballet, especially in the Elysian Fields, there was an almost celestial beauty, particularly in the pas de deux between Orpheus and Eurydice. In lighter vein there was her popular *Gods go a-Begging,* 1936, with its enchantment, gaiety and perfect period sense. This latter quality, in all her work, was again in full bloom in *The Prospect Before Us,* 1940, with its brilliant

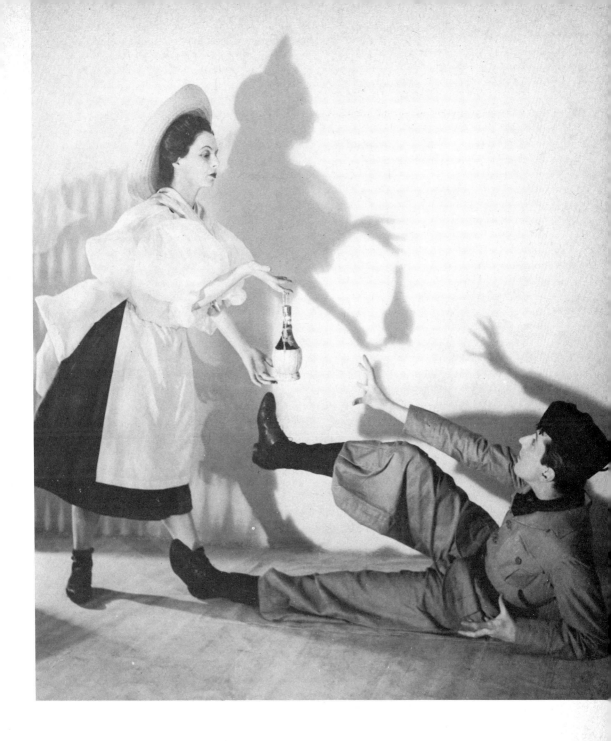

drunken dance which was outrageously funny whomsoever performed in it. In all, de Valois had over three score ballets to her credit, mostly during the poverty-stricken early days of the Vic-Wells. In 1933 she created the first choral ballet to be done

Ninette de Valois and Frederick Ashton in Barabau – the one occasion they danced together.

in England, namely *The Birthday of Oberon*, with music by Purcell arranged by Constant Lambert, and sets and costumes by John Armstrong. Here I quote from Edwin Evans, the leading music critic of the day: 'for beauty, imagination and variety Miss de Valois' choreography could scarcely have been bettered'. In 1934 she created *The Haunted Ballroom*, for some time a popular ballet, excitingly weird, sinister and at the same time very beautiful with its swiftly moving, swirling, ghostly figures. It was sad to see her give up, first her dancing then her choreography, especially as she had plans for two more works, but her first interest was the company. She would have needed all the energy, concentration, imagination and creative powers which she could ill-afford to spare in the terrific work of running the then considerably enlarged company, plus the school of ballet, lectures, rehearsals and general administration work. It was through the latter that we owe so much for the revival of the classics for which the company has a reputation of the highest standards today.

Since her retirement from directing the Royal Ballet in 1963 Dame Ninette turned her attention to the Royal Ballet schools; her garden of the Royal Ballet, where no doubt she did some planting, weeding and pruning until her final retirement from the organisation in 1972. However . . . old soldiers never die, they only fade away . . . so rumour has it that 'The Dame' is frequently seen—and heard—in and around the Royal Opera House when not flying off to her other National Ballet in Turkey, or reproducing her own ballets in various countries and continents.

In conclusion I am in full agreement with those who look upon Dame Ninette de Valois as one of the greatest pioneers in the history of ballet . . . who else has been a well known dancer, choreographer, teacher, lecturer, authoress, *and* the founder of two National Ballet Companies? So long may her finely sculptured head be seen in its place of honour on the grand staircase of the Royal Opera House, Covent Garden and at the Sadlers Wells Theatre.

2 Frederick Ashton

Frederick Ashton as Pierrot in Carnaval *seemed to portray a too pathetic rather than a wistful, slightly comic character.*

DURING A LONDON season in the mid-'twenties, I saw a pas de deux danced at a ball by an attractive debutante and a very slightly built young man. Little did I realise that I would marry the one, Frances James, and that the other, Frederick Ashton, was to become one of the world's most famous choreographers. Nor did I know that I would become a photographer and that for forty years I would have the pleasure of watching Ashton's career.

As a person he was shy and retiring, except at parties when he could be persuaded to become a mildly Carabossian mimic

—his impersonations ranged from Queen Victoria and Queen Alexandra to Ninette de Valois. I think it was this gift for mimicry which helped to build up his choreographic talents. Thus it was that in his early days one could recognise a Pavlova solo inserted into one of his own ballets. Like all creative artists, Ashton was influenced by his contemporaries. He

Frederick Ashton and Mollie Brown in the tango from Façade. *Molly Brown, a soloist of the company was a soubrette of great charm and vivacity.*

Frederick Ashton as the hussar in the ballroom scene from his own ballet Apparitions.

watched, listened, and absorbed ideas which were then re-modelled, improved and given added lustre and polish by being mounted in a choreographic setting of his own invention—in short, Ashton is like a choreographic oyster, a grain is inserted and out comes the perfect pearl. Ashton's love of the classics, his romanticism and musical phrasing are the cornerstones of his success and give to his work a distinction entirely his own. He has created over three score ballets for the company since he joined them as resident choreographer in 1935. He reminds me of the Charlatan in *Petrushka,* wafting his wand and weaving spells around his 'puppets'.

Before joining the company, Ashton had already created several ballets for them and many for Marie Rambert's Ballet Club; indeed it was Rambert who gave him his first commission to do a ballet for Nigel Playfair in 1926. Within five years he had created seven ballets at the Wells with leading roles for the young Fonteyn. In fact it may well be said that he created through his ballets—the pearl from the oyster!

Ballets such as *Baiser de la Fée* in 1935, *Apparitions* and

17

Nocturne, 1936, *A Wedding Bouquet,* 1937, *Horoscope,* 1938, *The Wise Virgins,* 1940, and *The Wanderer* in 1941. Since those days he has created at least twelve more for Fonteyn—including three of his finest works and her most rewarding roles in *Daphnis and Chloe, Ondine,* and *Marguerite and Armand.* *Horoscope* was one of Ashton's first important dramatic ballets for the Vic-Wells; its appeal was both musical and visual, having a score by Constant Lambert with costumes and decor by Sophie Fedorovitch whose understanding of ballet and dancers plus her general intelligence made her a very fine designer. Her simplicity, subtleties of design and costumes have never been bettered, and her tragic death in 1953 was a terrible loss to the company. In this ballet Ashton invented a lovely *pas de trois* for her as the Moon and the Gemini of slow movements and flowing lifts; the Gemini was danced by two young soloists, Alan Carter and Richard Ellis, both of whom themselves became principals of the company. Today Alan Carter is a well known choreographer, director, and an artist of considerable skill, and Richard Ellis runs a highly successful school of ballet in Chicago. This may seem irrelevant but in fact it demonstrates Ashton's foresight and surety of judgement concerning young dancers,

Ashton appears to me to be a very personal choreographer, getting inspiration from the material at hand, so his ballets fit both the style and technical accomplishments of his dancers— he creates from the concrete rather than from the abstract, and it is his intense sensitivity and understanding of music combined with his love of the romantic which makes his work at times so magical. The personal touch in those early days was particularly noticeable in the way he used Robert Helpmann in *A Wedding Bouquet* (the bridegroom), Michael Somes in *Horoscope,* Julia Farron in *Cupid and Psyche,* and Harold Turner in *Les Patineurs.* Two perfect examples in later years are the roles created for Svetlana Beriosova in *Persephone* and Nadia Nerina in *La Fille mal Gardée.*

In his own performances Ashton was more actor than dancer and I well remember his first performance as Pierrot in *Carnaval,* which I enjoyed but felt it stressed tragedy rather than the greater subtleties the role required. Indeed I have rarely seen this part played to perfection—Pierrot should only be pathetic to those who watch his foolish, pitiful gaiety, failing to grasp the hopeless moonshine desires of his life—a Chaplinesque character extremely hard to portray. Of all the other roles in

which I have seen him, among them the Tango in *Facade,*
Kostchei in the *Firebird,* the Charlatan in *Petrushka,* and
Carabosse in *The Sleeping Beauty,* there are none to touch his
now famous Ugly Sister in his own ballet *Cinderella.* Despite
its mad fooling, he drew a remarkably likeable and rather
pathetic portrait of the old girl.

To return to his choreography. His production of Elgar's
Enigma Variations has all one expects of an Ashton ballet—its
lovely, gentle, warm sense of period, elegance and wistfulness is
wafted across the footlights, engulfing us all with an Edwardian
nostalgia. One of Ashton's most important assets is his versatility. Take a glance at some of his works—the brilliant, satirical
frolic of *A Wedding Bouquet;* the robust and elegant Edwardian
farce of *Les Sirènes;* the frothy classical brilliance and gaiety of
Les Rendezvous; the profoundly moving musical perfection of
Symphonic Variations; the pantomime fun and charm of
Cinderella; the wit of *Facade;* the dramatic, Central European
style of *Dante Sonata;* the pure Victorian classicism of *Sylvia;*
and so on to the rhythmical, flowing plastic fluidity of *Mono-
tones.* Whether reviving the classics or in his own works,
Ashton has proved himself a fine producer while his pioneering
work for the company is inestimable.

The retirement of Sir Frederick Ashton from the director-
ship of the company in 1970 was a sad occasion for many but
I personally am happy to think that our greatest choreographer
will have more time to devote exclusively to his own work,
unhampered by a lot of irrelevant administration. I hope that
we have not yet seen the gamut of his creative genius. I had the
good fortune to see Ashton's creation for two young dancers,
Lament of the Waves, at the Gala performance in honour of his
retirement. This proved the fact that in this modern permissive
age and harsh idiom of the dance he can add his own romantic
and lyrical qualities, turning what might have been, possibly,
a long pas de deux of choreographic copulation into something
moving, memorable and lovely to look at. His superlative sense
of production as usual played a major role.

Since his retirement Sir Frederick has done little work of
note; no doubt he feels and knows that he has earned the right
to relax, the wisdom not to force himself when the natural flow
of imagination and inventiveness is on the wane . . . the spark
goes and fires only flicker. The 'legend' of Frederick Ashton and
his muse Margot Fonteyn will forever remain in the annals of
British ballet.

3 Beatrice Appleyard

A GREAT MANY English dancers lack the nervous sensitivity, both musical and mental, of their continental contemporaries which deprives them of the emotional power so necessary for highly dramatic roles and the building up of the characters they are portraying. This applies especially in the great classics—which provide no 'disguise' for the dancer to hide behind—but, on the other hand, the failing, if failing it is, in our dancers is offset to a great extent by their natural grace and gentle dignity and authority when they depict royalty on the stage. It is something very different from the exuberant arrogance of the Slav dancers—and I am thinking of the Ballets Russes dancers of the 'thirties as much as of the Bolshoi dancers of today—but something which I find remarkably attractive in the English school of ballet.

These English qualities, and some of the warmth of the Slavs, were particularly noticeable in the work of Beatrice Appleyard, one of Ninette de Valois' original pupils at her Academy of Dancing in Roland Gardens in the mid-'twenties and she became one of the first salaried members of the Vic-Wells company, although the salary was a mere pittance in comparison with what dancers earn today.

I watched Ninette de Valois in those early days give what she called *plastique* or composition classes. These were done in soft shoes—or no shoes, if the pupil forgot to bring them—and were simple, rhythmical movements based on the Dalcroze system. It was in ballets choreographically based on this system in which Beatrice Appleyard appeared to true advantage, rather than in the purely classical ballets. It is, therefore, reasonable that I should remember with special enjoyment her performances in some of de Valois' earlier works such as *Danse Sacrée et Danse Profane* and *The Scorpions of Ysitt*—the latter being produced for the first time on 15 November 1932. It was an amusing comedy ballet with a scenario by Terence Grey (the Egyptologist and director of the Festival Theatre, Cambridge) which concerned a marsh woman who, frightened by the attendant scorpions of the Goddess Ysitt, refuses the Goddess hospitality. This is given by a second marsh woman and the Goddess, in revenge, causes the scorpions to kill the first

Beatrice Appleyard as the farmer's daughter in The Jar *a light gay little role she danced with her usual grace and style.*

woman's baby. Eventually all ends in peace and forgiveness. As the creator of the role of the Goddess Ysitt in this ballet, Beatrice Appleyard was excellent and received much praise for her performance, which was full of the stylised grace and regal dignity demanded of her. I also found her to 'look' the part to perfection, with her finely modelled facial bone structure and lovely figure. The costumes and decor for this ballet were, incidentally, by Sophie Fedorovitch whose name is more often associated with that of Frederick Ashton and whose superb work meant so much to the company in later years. The music was specially composed by Gavin Gordon—later to write the music for *The Rake's Progress*.

Beatrice Appleyard's beauty was also ideally suited to the revival of Ashton's *Pomona* (first made for the Camargo Society in January 1933). This production had new costumes and decor by Vanessa Bell and through it Beatrice Appleyard moved with a fluidity and delicacy most pleasing to watch.

She also created other roles in de Valois' ballets, including that of the farmer's wife in *The Jar,* Beatrice in *The Haunted Ballroom* (the characters were named after their creators), and Lady Clara Vere de Vere in Ashton's *The Lord of Burleigh* (17 October 1932) with its new costumes and decor by George Sheringham.

During the teething years of the company there was often only one performance a week. Nevertheless the work entailed by the dancers was incredibly hard compared with today's streamlined organisation. While a member of the company— she left in 1935—Beatrice Appleyard was a soloist and principal dancer in innumerable ballets. I remember her Danse Arabe in the first production in England of *Casse Noisette,* produced in January 1934 by Nicholas Sergueff, with designs by Hedley Briggs. The solo was an amusing one, a pseudo-Ouled Nail belly dance, rightly appreciated by myself and the audience but frowned on by Ninette de Valois as 'Music Hall'. It was!

Beatrice Appleyard left the Wells to join the Markova-Dolin company and then entered the commercial theatre. In 1951 she did further pioneering for de Valois by working with the Turkish National Ballet until 1954 when she left to open her own Conservatoire in Ankara. She is married to a Turk and Turkey is now her home. But to have been instrumental in the pioneering work of two national ballet companies is a rare achievement and surely the hallmark of a successful career.

4 Pearl Argyle

Pearl Argyle in Le Roi Nu *showing her fine bone structure and modelling of great beauty.*

THE TWO MOST beautiful women of all the theatre, opera, ballet and socialite people who came to my studio were Vivien Leigh and Pearl Argyle. Curiously both their looks and careers were rather similar—although Pearl's was sadly shortened by her sudden death in 1947. They only had to set foot on the stage and one 'felt' the audience falling into a sort of coma of delight! They both had fabulous reputations beyond their actual technical abilities. This is not meant derogatively, but to point out a rare and enviable asset, the victory of personality and artistry over workmanship.

Before Pearl Argyle joined the Vic-Wells company in 1935—first as a guest artist and later, in 1936, as premiere danseuse—she already had a renowned professional reputation having danced for the Camargo Society for Balanchine's Ballets 1933 and also creating several roles for Frederick Ashton with Marie Rambert—to whom she owed her initial training (like many others who graduated into the company). Furthermore, she had some films to her credit—such as *Things to Come*—besides working in the commercial theatre for Cochrane among others. Pearl Argyle had the cool creamy beauty of a real pearl with its 'lustre' in her large expressive eyes. In her classical work she had the nobility and serenity of a true ballerina and in modern ballets both a chic and sophisticated quality comparatively rare in those early days of the company. This particularly appealed to the 'smart set' and to the socialites of the day, as well as to the general public and helped to increase the popularity of the company. Her personality, like her character, was gentle but firm, getting over to her audiences, whereas many with stronger personalities off stage failed to do this. She had the star quality without its 'twinkle' which, to me, always savours of tinsel and the circus, excellent maybe in the right type. The Russians, for instance, adore it and it does suit their naturally more volatile temperament. One contemporary critic described Pearl Argyle as of 'great beauty and exquisite sensitivity' and after her first performance as Columbine in *Carnaval* another stated that 'the young company had lost a Markova and gained a Pearl Argyle'. This was hardly surprising, for her predecessor, Markova, was not in my opinion so well suited to this role. One finds Arnold Haskell stating that she had 'translated a natural reserve into true serenity' and it was this that so enriched many of her performances—especially in the classical repertoire.

Between 1935 and 1938 Pearl Argyle danced many leading ballets including *Les Sylphides, Carnaval, Baiser de la Fée, The Gods go a'Begging, The Lord of Burleigh, Facade, Le Roi Nu, Pomona* and Ashton's *The Judgement of Paris*. She also had the distinction of being the first English dancer to dance the famous Aurora pas de deux for the company or, indeed, in England. It was taught to her and Robert Helpmann by Sergueff especially for the company. In this her beauty, poise, musical sensitivity and 'grand manner' gave us our first taste, apart

24

from Markova, of the forthcoming English tradition of a prima ballerina assoluta growing up from within the company itself.

However, I remember her mostly in the modern ballets and above all her creation of the fairy in Frederick Ashton's *Baiser de la Fée* in 1936. This eerie ballet is about a fairy who finds a woman and her male baby lost in snowbound woods; she plants a kiss on his brow and many years later returns to claim him for her own upon his wedding day taking him with her to the land of snow and ice. I remember how well she depicted the strange, sinister, cold beauty and aloofness of the fairy, which seemed to permeate the whole atmosphere. The ballet was beautifully mounted, too, with decor and costumes by Sophie Federovitch. Ashton's choreography suited Pearl perfectly, as he was already becoming a master in the art of creating roles for his dancers. In this ballet, too, he wrote a lovely pas de deux for young Margot Fonteyn and Harold Turner.

However, Pearl's very first creation with the Company was the serving maid in Ninette de Valois' *The Gods go a'Begging*. This ballet about a God and Goddess disguising themselves as servants and joining the mortals in a *fête champêtre* to music by Handel, Fragonard settings by Hugh Stevenson and costumes by William Chappell. It was a small masterpiece of period, eighteenth century French elegance and gay fantasy completely different from the Ashton ballet. Here, indeed, the other side of her work appeared: gone was the coldness of the fairy queen; it was supplanted by the delicacy of feeling and warmth of the veritable Goddess of Beauty she represented. Again the role was choreographically tailormade to suit her, and she proved most worthy of it. But it was so charming that many of her successors were delightful in it.

There is no doubt that Pearl Argyle's previous experience and professionalism were of great help to the young company, and it was a considerable loss when she married film producer Kurt Bernhardt and went to live in America. She will always be remembered with admiration by those who knew her work and with great affection by those who knew her personally. In an obituary notice Marie Rambert quoted from *The Lady of Shallot* (which Pearl danced for her at the Ballet Club): 'She had a lovely face . . . God in his mercy send her grace.'

5 June Brae

WHENEVER THE WORD June is mentioned one inevitably thinks of that elusive English summer. Hot, sunny days with starlit and romantic nights, when everyone seems happy with warmth and friendship abounding. That describes June Brae to perfection both in her work and her personality, with perhaps an occasional thunderstorm to clear the air!

Having said that, it seems rather comical that most of her major creations were ladies of decidedly doubtful character and intent. The 'Other Woman' in Ninette de Valois' *Prometheus* (1936), was her first creative role with the company, and a delightful piece of *baggagerie* she made it. In contrast the role of the Black Queen which she created for de Valois' *Checkmate* (1937) was a superb characterization of a chessboard Messalina. A further contrast in her work was in Frederick Ashton's *Nocturne* as the Rich Girl, a chic performance of a lady with obvious charms and sophisticated allurement. In the same year she created the Leader of the Children of Darkness in Ashton's *Dante Sonata*. In this Central European style barefoot ballet, the fury of her wild and frenzied movements were the epitome of evil, something out of Hades that might have made even Satan blush. The sensuality of *Checkmate* was replaced by pure animal agility and viciousness. A further change of character was shown as Josephine in Ashton's *A Wedding Bouquet,* when she created that delightfully tipsy character. It was a delectable performance of alcoholic abandonment which she spiced with a monstrous, middle-class, delicate English innocent charm.

June's versatility covered many different types of solos as well as leading roles. I remember particularly well her Prayer in *Coppelia,* with its deep poetic, religious feeling. Some years later Andrée Howard created *Assembly Ball* for her to Bizet's Symphony in C, in 1946. This ballet with its lightness, exuberance and gaiety suited her own personality so well. It was the ballet which brought her the greatest reclame from a purely dancing point of view.

Perhaps the most satisfying role of all for her, shortly before she retired, was in Robert Helpmann's *Adam Zero,* at Covent Garden in 1946. Here I quote a contemporary critic . . . And it

June Brae in Checkmate *in which she gave a seductively cruel portrayal of great quality as 'The black queen'.*

propensities . . .

I have rushed ahead and now return to the pioneering days when she joined the company in 1935 as June Bear. However, ran the full length of her dramatic as well as dancing

June Brae as Josephine in A Wedding Bouquet. *She gave a highly amusing performance of a typical Edwardian maudlin 'miss'.*

de Valois didn't care for the idea of performing bears in her company so changed it to Brae. As a child she trained in China at the same school as Margot Fonteyn and in England with Legat, and Paris with Kchessinska, after which she became a student of the ballet company in 1933. She danced in many of the classics and was the Lilac Fairy in the first production by Nicholas Sergueff of *The Sleeping Beauty,* then known as *The Sleeping Princess,* in 1939. The company was so much smaller then that many of the fairies had to double roles. June had the distinction of being the first English dancer to dance the Lilac Fairy and she was the essence of graceful charm and authoritative dignity. By nature she was a gentle person, and that is perhaps why I found her so very delightful as the Young Girl in *Spectra de la Rose,* which she danced with Alexis Rassine in 1944.

As with Pearl Argyle, June Brae was another of those cases where, technically not very strong, she overcame this by her individuality and a sort of 'star' quality. Added to this she had a very wide field of dramatic capabilities, which she used to great advantage. The only major classical role she performed was Giselle, in Leeds during the war. A first, and naturally tentative, performance by a young dancer, whose technique was more modern than classical, it inevitably had its short-comings, but one was very aware of her potentialities. I was more satisfied with her than with many more accomplished performances I had seen by other, stronger ballerinas.

In the 'thirties, one hardly ever thought of the company without the names of their three most popular stars, Fonteyn, May, Brae. It was sad that June didn't dance Giselle in London, but she had by then married and the birth of her first child prevented it. Shortly afterwards she retired although she made a brief 'come back' after the war to dance with the Sadler's Wells Theatre Ballet and at Covent Garden. Many of us still think with nostalgia and very great admiration, both of her as a personality and a dancer during the eleven years she so loyally served the company.

6 William Chappell

'BILLY' CHAPPELL IN his own individual way is a Jack of all trades and master of many. Dancer, scenic artist, dress designer, producer, choreographer and author. I do not remember his ever having a flop with any of the sixteen ballets he designed for the company, in many of which he also danced during the years between 1931 and 1940. In fact, what with his dancing and his designing, I think the ballet should have worn him out even more than the war years. But he always came out on top, bouncing about like a cork on troubled waters. All Billy's work during that period, particularly his decor and costume designs, were a reflection of himself—completely charming, easy on the eye, no hard, startling colours or brilliant contrasts ever used. When he had good reasons to be upset, there would be none of the usual temperamental explosions; only a sort of gentle wail came into his voice like a mild factory siren. He was a most valuable asset to the company.

Chappell was another product of Marie Rambert's ballet nursery. My first memory of him was in *L'Apres midi d'un faune* at the Ballet Club some time before he joined the company. It was an exciting evening as he was the first English dancer to tackle this role. I thought his performance was critically disarming, for this faune was so very young, enchanting and lovely to watch. But the soft, pulsating undercurrent of sensuality and physical desire of the music was missing; he appeared quite happy to possess the scarf instead of the nymph and really this was not quite the point. (I saw David Lichine do this ballet later—and no wonder the nymph dropped her scarf and ran!) However, as one critic stated, Chappell's was 'a performance of touching and moving adolescence by a lovely youth of delightful and pleasing artistry.'

Even before he entered the company, Chappell had done the sets and costumes for Ninette de Valois' *Cephalus and Procris*, created for the Camargo Society in 1931 and for its revival in the same year at the Old Vic. It is interesting to note that he also did the sets and costumes for *Narcissus and Echo* created by Ninette de Valois for Markova's first appearance with the Company as guest artist in 1932.

Chappell danced many leading roles including The Man in

30

de Valois' ballet *La Creation du Monde,* and a sailor in Ashton's *Rio Grande,* in which he danced opposite the young Fonteyn in her first role with the company in 1935. He also had many principal roles in ballets for which he did the decor and costumes including *Regatta* for de Valois at the Old Vic in 1931. This was quickly followed by *Les Rendezvous* 1933, *The Jar* 1934, *Les Patineurs* 1937, *The Judgement of Paris* 1938. This says much for his multiformity and characterization. His portrayal of Elihu in de Valois' *Job* could not have illustrated better the words 'for I am young and ye are very old.' As the young God in de Valois' *The Gods go a'Begging,* which he created for her in 1936, he gave a performance of enchantment and simplicity in complete harmony with his surroundings. Likewise in another important role which he created for de Valois as the Friend in *The Rake's Progress;* he appeared an integral part of the whole yet stood out with distinction and discretion. It was an ideal conception of an irresponsible eighteenth century 'Macaroni'. Both in the gambling and brothel scenes he managed to 'throw off' a comical sort of preening, bibulous elegance, and in the Bedlam scene his dance with a pack of cards, with its vague twisting, shuffling meanderings and head scratchings, might have meant little with a lesser artist. But he gave to it a horrible sort of vacuity, indigenous to certain types of mental cases—comic, sad, and horrific at the same time.

For de Valois' *Haunted Ballroom,* as the Strange Player dancing with a flute, with swirling, gracefully gliding movements, he succeeded in putting over an eerie feeling of the grey world between life and death.

I have already mentioned the ballets for which Chappell was both a soloist and scenic artist but there were many others in which he danced including *Facade, The Emperor's New Clothes, Checkmate,* and *Casse Noisette.* As the Lord of Burleigh in the ballet of that name by Frederick Ashton, at the Old Vic in 1932, in a shoulder length blonde wig he was the very presence of Victorian poesies.

It was sad when the war and call-up came along, but at least it has left behind for us two of his most delightful and typical works in *Les Patineurs* and *Les Rendezvous.* His two classical ballets, *Giselle* and *Coppelia* were among the mainstays of the repertory for many years.

When writing about such people as Billy Chappell I am apt to get a scatty attack of sentimentality for those far off, struggling and most admirable pioneering days, and for the artists who made it all so very worth while.

Since the war William Chappell has concentrated mainly on the commercial theatre, producing plays, cabarets, musicals and also writing. John Lehmann published his ballet criticism in *Penguin New Writing* and he went on to do excellent books, *Studies in Ballet* and *Margot Fonteyn*.

William Chappell as Elihu in Job. *He danced this elegiac solo with musicality and harmonious grace.*

7 Anton Dolin

PATRICK HEALEY-KAYE was born Irish by the grace of God in 1904 and re-born Anton Dolin by the grace of Serge Diaghilev in 1932. Most Irishmen are said to have kissed the blarney stone but Pat Dolin didn't have to—he *was* it! He would have danced, charmed and chortled his way out of hell itself if necessary, and in fact there never was a better Satan, the role he created for Ninette de Valois' *Job* in 1931. In a flaming red wig, his muscles accentuated by make-up, and his body of a slimy greenish hue, he ripped, leapt, stamped and slashed his way across the stage with an horrific and terrifying evil virile arrogance. One felt that Death himself would have cringed before embracing such a 'thing'. It is an extremely difficult role, as Satan's performance must dominate the whole ballet, and the ingenious choreography, particularly in his solo, can easily be blurred unless interpreted correctly, physically and mentally.

Dolin's fine physical strength added to his technical qualities, both as dancer and actor, made him one of the most out-standing dancers of our epoch. His work for the young company, both as principal guest artist and teacher, during his association with it on and off between 1931 and 1935 gave tremendous help and encouragement—particularly to the male dancers in those formative years. It was a weaning period for them, when parents in all walks of life frowned at and some screamed at the very thought of their son dancing. So those we had were sorely lacking in the basic training they get today. Dolin helped to give them a sense of the real importance of first class male dancing. I often wonder what would have happened in the Old Vic days without the help of guest artists and part-time principals in the company, such as Stanley Judson, who created Elihu in *Job*, Hedley Briggs our first Dr. Coppelius and scenic designer, and Stanislas Idzikovski, who gave the company its first taste of the Bluebird pas de deux, and Harlequin in *Carnaval*. But it was Dolin in *Giselle* and *Swan Lake* who set the seal of the future high standard of classical ballet the company later achieved.

Dolin created two minor roles for the company, one for de Valois in *Douanes,* and the other for Frederick Ashton in *The Lord of Burleigh,* both of which were in 1932. *Douanes,* with music by Geoffrey Toye and decor by Hedley Briggs, was a gay bit of witty triviality about a tight-rope walker (de Valois) and a Customs officer danced by Dolin, in which his usual quick, slick, energetic movements were well synchronised with de Valois' deliciously amusing flirtatious philanderings as the tight-rope walker. They seemed to vie with each other in turning an *hors d'oeuvre* into a minor banquet with a photo finish! *The Lord of Burleigh* was a charming, nostalgic Victorian trifle with music by Mendelssohn, arranged by Constant Lambert, and equally effective costumes by George Sherringham. In this ballet, Dolin had a romantic role and dance on classical lines well suited to his abundant fund of showmanship.

Now to go back to the classics, the first of which was *Spectre de la Rose* in 1932, danced with Ninette de Valois. This was a disappointment. De Valois was disappointing, too. Both her personality and mentality were ill-suited to the sentimental romanticism demanded by the role. Technically Dolin was fine but much too human; this muscularly controlled, handsome young athlete, covered in rather fleshy rosebuds, failed to project the illusions of a young girl's dream world, leaving only the bare realities of this very solid earth, despite his remarkable ballon. Similarly with the finale of the famous mad scene in *Giselle,* he failed in his emotional impact on me despite a flawless performance. The fact is that Dolin always used the cloak of romanticism with dignity, distinction and to very great effect, but the romantic and dramatic highlights would become veiled in the mists of his fundamental practicality. The magic touch was missing. Thus, despite his phenomenal success in the classics, I always preferred his modern works where his good looks, electrical personality and physique, added to his technical prowess and showmanship, harmonized into a perfect whole as in *Le Bal, Le Train Bleu* and *Les Biches* for Diaghilev; *David,* with Keith Lester's choreography for the Markova-Dolin company; *Les Présages* and *The Prodigal Son,* for de Basil.

I first met Pat at a rehearsal in Monte Carlo when visiting my sister, Ninette de Valois, in 1923. At that time, she, Dolin and Markova were new to the Diaghilev company and the latter two were the great man's latest 'finds'. He himself was watching a rehearsal, so a reverential silence was a very definite order of the day—the kind you can almost hear. I shall never forget the half amused and half fearful agitation shown by my sister to whom Pat chose to gossip in very Irish stage whispers (far louder than most). Luckily for her, something she said, which I didn't hear, turned Pat off like an electric switch. The

Anton Dolin in Job. *He gave a violently malevolent performance as Satan never beaten or forgotten.*

34

Irish certainly know how to obliterate each other! He was very young then and I was very impressed by his remarkable energy, sense of fun and general *joie de vivre*. It was easy to see he was difficult to control; in fact the only completely controlled thing about Dolin was his dancing, which was even then quite astoundingly good and it is not surprising that he became Britain's first world-renowned male dancer.

It is most pleasing to realise that Dolin's excellent pioneering work for the company was fully rewarded by Ninette de Valois' revivals of *Swan Lake* and *Giselle,* which she had produced for him and Markova by Nicholas Sergueff. Since that time the names of these two classics of the ballet have become synonymous with the names of these first two English internationally famous dancers.

Anton Dolin in Spectre de la rose *a vital virile performance but Dolin was of the earth earthy . . . the 'spectre' was missing.*

8 Leslie Edwards

Leslie Edwards as the old beggar in The Gorbals. *A fine demonstration of a drunken fiddler tottering around from one garbage-bin to another watching the life of teeming sordidity around him.*

As ONE OF the Royal Ballet's first actor-dancers, Leslie Edwards, during the course of some forty years, has represented almost everything from the tail of a cow in *Facade* to Carabosse in the *Sleeping Beauty,* and yet the name of this fine and reliable artist means little to some balletomanes and almost nothing to the general rank and file of ballet audiences. It is a depressing thought that in ballet histories one reads too much about the few and too little about the many—and what's the use of an obituary notice to the living?

The actor-dancer usually starts life, as Edwards did, as a soloist or in the corps de ballet, developing through various stages to demi-character and character dancing, gradually ceasing all actual dancing and concentrating entirely upon mime roles. These artists are one of the main arteries in the life blood of a ballet company, and far too little recognition is given to their work, by critics and audiences alike. They are taken for granted. I once overheard a conversation on these lines, 'and how's poor old Leslie? . . . why, what's the matter with him?, oh, *nothing*!' Actually 'poor old Leslie' was happily rich both in health and talent. I attribute this remark to an attitude of mind towards the actor-dancer at that time which I found a disgrace to one's intelligence and insulting to the artist. It ignores the tremendous importance of their work, especially when you remember, as I do, how much the ballet suffered in its early days from the lack of mature artists, the Queen Mother often being younger than her Princeling son and so on.

I think this is how such roles become, in the general public's mind, relegated to the 'attics' of the ballet's assets, and the stigma seems to linger on in some odd and crazy way. Anyway I am digressing badly, as usual, so let's get back to Leslie Edwards with his successful and at times inspired performances. I say this because some of his work was just that. I shall never forget a gem of a character sketch in his delightfully endearing portrayal of the beggar in Robert Helpmann's *Miracle in the Gorbals*. He meandered about the dustbins with his violin, a tragic, touching figure who seemed to have a religious understanding and acceptance of the sordid maelstrom of sleazy life seething around him; a minor part truly, but it moved me quite remarkably. Here I would like to mention a few more of the many diversified roles Leslie Edwards has done for the company during his long association with them—The Red King in de Valois' *Checkmate,* Archimado in Ashton's *The Quest,* Don Quixote for de Valois, a religious and kindly Quaker sea captain in Andrée Howard's *Mirror for Witches,* the old farmer in Ashton's *La Fille mal Gardee,* the Archbishop in Helpmann's *Adam Zero,* Hilarion in *Giselle,* Catallabutte and Carabosse in the *Sleeping Beauty.* I much regret not seeing his Carabosse, but his creation of Catallabutte for the 1946 version of *The Sleeping Beauty* was a needlelike characterisation of a court official with his unctuous servility towards his superiors, and showing an elegantly grand pomposity to his inferiors. It was a perfect parody of the natural dignity and graciousness of his

Leslie Edwards as Archimado in The Quest. *An excellent example of conventional lines of diabolic priestcraft.*

royal master and mistress. What a contrast was this to his pathetic old king in de Valois' *Checkmate,* his slightly quaint, rather comic necromancing as Dr Coppelius, and the monstrously evil necromancing of his Archimado in Ashton's *The Quest.* A further contrast was his broadly comic, Falstaffian figure as Thomas the farmer in Ashton's *La Fille mal Gardee.* He played the king in *The Sleeping Beauty*—in fact I wouldn't be surprised to hear he had even played the Queen Mother in *Swan Lake,* thereby completing the succession of his royal, civic and ecclesiastical roles, both sacred and profane.

Leslie Edwards was born in London in 1916 and had his early training with Marie Rambert, joining the Vic-Wells company in 1933. The first time I remember seeing him was as Florestan in *Carnaval,* which he danced in 1935, then in *Facade* and later in de Valois' *The Rake's Progress* in 1935, in which he created four different character sketches, the Musician, a Creditor, a Gambler and the King in the Bedlam scene. In *Checkmate,* he started as a Red Castle, later a Red Knight and finally the Red King himself—quite a progress in one ballet! However, his creation for Ashton as Archimado in *The Quest* was his first all important role and he received universal praise. His was the success, not the ballet, and it set the seal for his future. To this day Leslie Edwards is still being enjoyed for his character studies in the Royal Ballet, in such works as *Enigma Variations* and *Romeo and Juliet.* On top of all this he has been for some years one of the company's repetiteurs and is extremely busy with his successful Royal Ballet Choreographic Group; he is also an artist and director of the Opera Ballets. This he created in 1967 for the encouragement of future dancers and, especially, choreographers under the auspices of The Friends of Covent Garden. Already, we owe a great deal to him for two of our most promising young choreographers in David Drew and Geoffrey Cauley.

And now one can fervently hope that, with the disbandment of the Royal Ballet touring company, Leslie Edwards with his Choreographic Group will be given still greater scope to develop his latest—and perhaps greatest—triumph of pioneering work with the Royal Ballet. As the Astronauts say, keep going, you're looking good!

9 Julia Farron

IN THE FIRMAMENT there are countless twinkling stars of various sizes, and as a child I had often been struck by the sight of a small but extra bright one. Julia Farron is just such a one in the ever increasing galaxy of ballet stars. Artists of her calibre are invaluable to their companies. They are not ballerinas yet way above the ordinary soloist, and many are quite capable of accepting the occasional ballerina role. In fact they are principal dancers with a wide range, known as character and demi-character dancers, but unfortunately they miss a lot of the literary acclaim handed out to their more fortunate colleagues, which would appear unfair and unrealistic. However, the very great quantity of their roles is inclined to blur the issue critically, especially as many of them are of comparatively minor importance in proportion to the whole. In fact their accumulative work is kaleidoscopic: they are to ballet as the precious and semi-precious stones surrounding the centre gem of a ring.

'Joyce' Farron was born of English parents in London in 1922. She had her early training at the Cone School, from which she won, in 1931, the first scholarship to the Vic-Wells Ballet School, itself in its infancy, from which she graduated into the company. Her name was later changed to Julia Farron. I remember very well Joyce Farron as Little Bo-Peep in de Valois' *Nursery Suite,* Clara in *Casse Noisette* and, particularly, her first impact as the little dog Pepé in Ashton's *A Wedding Bouquet*. However, it was her Psyche which she created for Ashton's *Cupid and Psyche* in 1939, that really shook me. The ballet itself, despite some charming and delightful music and designs by Lord Berners and Sir Francis Rose, was a bad flop. Farron made a personal success, indeed she was quite breath-taking and her youthfulness, fluidity of line, speed and considerable technique made one look forward to a possible future ballerina assoluta. However, old mother fate in her ham-fisted way decided otherwise, and she became a brilliant demi-character dancer taking over many leading roles (apart from creating others) mainly in modern ballets, such as the Girl in *The Rake's Progress,* in which I found her so typically English. Her interpretation was more formal but just as moving as her predecessor, Mary Honer, perhaps even more so for that very reason.

Farron's performance as Alicia in de Valois' *The Haunted Ballroom* was not ethereal like that of its originator, Alicia Markova; she gave to it an almost vicious attack, instead of creating a slightly sinister atmosphere—Markova an ectoplasm, Farron a poltergeist. They were both excellent on their own astral plane!

Julia Farren as Alicia in The Haunted Ballroom. *Inheriting the role from Markova. Very lovely and exciting, but nobody ever had Markova's incorperiality.*

Another important take-over was Mlle Théodore in de Valois' *The Prospect Before Us,* and this too was most successful, equal in fact to that made by its creator, Pamela May. Julia used her captivating smile, intelligence and refreshing personality to great effect. The performance was fickle, frothy and capricious; one could well imagine her throwing away her protector, almost a point of honourable dishonour in those days, as gaily as she did her ill-fitting ballet shoes at the commencement of her first solo.

Much later on, I found myself enjoying a very different and more dramatic role, that of the Red Queen in *Checkmate.* In the original production, Pamela May was the Red Queen and Joyce Farron a Red Pawn. I thought her performance was totally suited to the architecturally stylized dramatic choreography and she succeeded in bringing out enough of the human drama with her gentle, loving, sensitive handling of the Old King.

Her classical solos, which included the Diamond Fairy, Breadcrumb Fairy (the finger variation) in the company's original production of *The Sleeping Princess* in 1939 suited her clear sparkling technique, remarkable speed and musicality. I have seen her 'tear the house down' in Ashton's Tarantella in *Le Lac des Cygnes,* no matter who partnered her. Incidentally I have never seen the Tarantella in *La Boutique Fantastique* danced with such verve and precision, except by its famous originator, Lydia Sokolova.

Julia Farron's very strong personality, coupled as it is with good clear miming and her sense of theatre, has turned her into one of the Company's finest artists in acting roles. In ballets such as Andrée Howard's *Mirror for Witches,* and Ashton's *Ondine,* she gave performances of which any *actress* could be proud. As Carabosse in a previous production of *The Sleeping Beauty* she created an astonishingly spiteful incarnation of witchcraft, despite a crazily comic unwieldy crocodile's tail.

I cannot end without mentioning Farron's performance as the Prostitute in Helpmann's *Miracle in the Gorbals.* It showed a depth of understanding that softened the dreary brashness of the character.

Despite Julia Farron's work on the teaching staff of the Royal Ballet School, she still finds time to be a most welcome guest artist. I for one look forward to seeing her wear for many years her lovely court gowns with her gracious and Royal dignity.

OF ALL THE great dancers I have seen, including Adeline Genée, Pavlova, Karsavina, Spessivtzeva, Markova, Ulanova, and many modern ones, Dame Margot Fonteyn stands alone on a pinnacle. Naturally, it might be thought by some that I am prejudiced in her favour for I had known and photographed her for close on thirty years, from her earliest days as a coryphée in 1935, produced three books about her, and had a long and happy friendship with her and her family. Her brother, Felix, as a youth was apprenticed to me. This close association does not in any way affect my judgement, for I am a very critical person, especially where friends and relations are concerned, being, I suppose, over-anxious on their behalf. However, nobody is perfect, and I have sometimes seen Fonteyn miscast, having in mind such ballets as Ashton's *Scènes de Ballet* and Balanchine's *Ballet Imperial,* with their rather speedy, staccato and sometimes angular movements, very much at variance with her natural flow of movement and very humanely warm personality.

Many people wonder how it is that Margot Fonteyn retained her title as the world's greatest ballerina for so long, for she won the crown as long ago as the first American tour in 1949. Of course there are, and have been, many ballerinas of greater technical ability, but she retained enough of that, while her ever-increasing artistry and dramatic powers kept her where she was and continued to do so.

Margot Fonteyn's major roles have varied from *Coppelia* and all the greater classics, including the modern ballets—Ashton's *Daphnis and Chloe, Ondine, Cinderella,* and MacMillan's superb production of *Romeo and Juliet,* to the almost off-beat creation of Roland Petit's *Paradise Lost,* and his more nebulous *Pelleas and Melisande.* In all she has created over two dozen major roles, and been prima ballerina for the company in many others in addition to the classics already mentioned. Surely this record has not been surpassed by any other living ballerina, especially for one company.

There is an illusive quality about Fonteyn's work which puzzled me for ages, and one day after watching a performance of *Ondine* I decided that this was one of the secrets of her success, and that it lay in her subconscious self. Ondine was a

Margot Fonteyn in A Wedding Bouquet *as the semi-mental Julia. . . . The first chance she had of showing wit and humour adding just the right amount of pathos.*

water sprite who emerges from a lake to lead an intensely human, emotional life, which tragically ends in her death and return to the depth of the lake. The interpretation of this role struck me as being 'her', a highly sensitive, chameleon-like creature of beauty, gaiety, warmth, passion and great generosity, with a dangerously innocent wayward sense of living, the latter exemplified by her childish amusement in rocking and wrecking the boat in the second scene. It moved me terribly, and I think it is such qualities in her which bubble to the surface bringing her portrayals to life more than those of all other dancers, in such roles as Odette-Odile, Aurora, Giselle and Juliet, in fact all of her roles requiring romanticism and drama. They were particularly noticeable in Frederick Ashton's *Daphnis and Chloe,* from her first childlike, carefree, adolescent gaiety through the virginal horrors and pleadings of her captivity, to the gentle 'river of love' flowing from her in the last act pas de deux, and on to the ecstatically purely physical excitement of the Coda.

I have chosen photographs mainly of roles created by Fonteyn during the first ten years of the company. As the principal picture I have used one of her first Giselles in 1937, when she was seventeen, for of all her classical roles this has been her only really controversial one. I consider her earliest and latest performances the most rewarding. This proves my theory that Giselle, like Hamlet, can best be played by a youngster of astounding abilities, or by a mature artist; the in-between years are sticky until intellect, dramatic abilities and technique are fully matured and synchronised. This, in my opinion, is exactly what happened to Fonteyn, who eventually took her place in the tradition of truly great Giselles.

Margot Fonteyn's range of classical roles is phenomenal when one stops to consider them. The diverse characterisations needed and fully developed by her in *The Sleeping Beauty, Giselle, Swan Lake, Casse Noisette, Sylvia,* and *The Firebird.* This last ballet is the shortest and in some ways the most lovely of them all, and it is very difficult to interpret the subtleties and strange nuances and mysteries of the shimmering Stravinsky score. Nobody, except, I imagine, Karsavina, who created the role for Diaghilev and taught it to Fonteyn, could explore so sensuously and sensitively the strange and weirdly beautiful 'mesmerizing to sleep' of Kotchei's creatures, with its wonderful flow of soothing, quivering music.

No dancer has ever created such a furore for so many years as she has done. As Juliet in Kenneth Macmillan's exacting and exciting ballet she filled famous opera houses to capacity as late as 1973. Of course Fonteyn's technique dropped severely, but was much counterbalanced by her acting abilities, sheer personal magic, and excellent musicality.

In 1970 I saw Fonteyn dance at the Gala tribute to Frederick Ashton's retirement; it was uncanny to see her wistful little solo from *Nocturne* which she first danced in 1936 . . . she not only appeared about seventeen but managed to convey the bewildered look of suffering with marvellous economy of gestures.

As a person she is elusive and enigmatic, being a mixture of

Margot Fonteyn in Giselle, aged seventeen. Her extreme youth, natural sense of drama, romanticism, musicality and dawning magical personality stifled all serious criticism.

46

Margot Fonteyn and Harold Turner in Baiser de la Fee. *She had already. shown her capacity for acting in* The Haunted Ballroom. *From gaiety to pathos she was in complete control of herself.*

romanticism, passion, mad gaiety, sensitivity, and exceptional generosity . . . shot through with a streak of steel. She is already spoken of as a legend and controversy rages round her; however, someone of fifty-four who can dance and act a girl of sixteen with considerable conviction is truly a 'phenomenon' . . . the 'legend' will follow.

Margot Fonteyn gave her last performance at Covent Garden early in 1974 but announced that she would appear for a time on the continents, 'the song is ended but the memory lingers on' . . . I can only add that one hopes the Royal Ballet will for ever be proud of having produced from its ranks a 'legend'.

48

11 Robert Helpmann

A MAN OF the theatre; Robert Helpmann came from a pioneering
stock and, typical of him, did a 'double take' by pioneering back
into his mother country as a dancer from Australia. One might
say that Helpmann's career was born of Pavlova, with whose
company he had his earliest experience, and weaned and
brought up by de Valois, who gave him his first major role as
Satan in *Job*, following Dolin in 1934. Although then not equal
to his famous predecessor, he gave an astoundingly good
performance with an entirely different approach, which brought
him almost hysterical applause. Dolin the tiger, Helpmann the
snake, and there you have it! One could imagine Dolin's Satan
battering on the gates of heaven and Helpmann slithering
through a crack in the door. In a similar way when Helpmann
took over the name part in *The Rake's Progress* from its creator
Walter Gore, he made of it a superb creation entirely his own
and to this day the ballet is associated with his name. However,
I found that Harold Turner who created the Dancing Master
and the horrific Man With The Rope in the original version
was 'dynamically' superior, though lacking in Helpmann's
subtleties and breadth of characterisation.

Bobby, as he is known by associates and friends, is a brilliantly
witty, amusingly wicked, raconteur and an impersonator who
pulls few, if any, stops. An expert mime and clown—a twentieth
century Grimaldi—he certainly has no equal in this country, if
anywhere. These gifts reached a peak in his hilariously funny
and lovable portrait of Dr Coppelius, now famous, which he
created in 1940. He no doubt upset the dramatic balance of the
ballet; however, as the latitude of genius knows no horizons, it
just didn't matter.

Among the several humorous roles created by him for the
company, was Mr O'Reilly in de Valois' *The Prospect Before
Us* in 1940. This was a quite outrageously, crazily, comic
character but in complete keeping with the role de Valois
created for him, a role dominating the whole ballet. It reached
its peak in his solo as a depressed, hysterically drunken Irish-
man, a magnificent performance of wit and zany farce topped
with the frothiest touch of a slightly pathetic quality, executed
with a terrific vitality and characterisation.

Helpmann created his first humorous character, the Bridegroom in *A Wedding Bouquet*, in 1936, for Frederick Ashton, a subtle and witty Edwardian pastiche. However, his creation in 1950, as the foil to Ashton's Ugly Sister in *Cinderella* still remains a masterpiece of pure slapstick, still delighted in by his audiences on his guest performances. His Ugly Sister is an impossibly mad, big, blustering bully of a beldam, with just the right touches of appalling coyness, the whole garnished with a mere wisp of pathos at the end: superb clowning.

Helpmann became one of the best *danseurs nobles* of his generation. His dancing, though lacking a strong technique, was smooth and lyrical with a certain ballon, and a remarkably easy, almost feline, grace; his miming was excellent. His parterning was always romantic, sympathetic, completely reliable and chivalrous to watch. Helpmann had the distinction of being the first British dancer to dance the role of the Prince in *The Sleeping Beauty,* and later on that of Carabosse. His charming, elegant and romantic Prince brilliantly contrasted

Robert Helpmann as Mr O'Reilly in the drunken dance from The Prospect Before Us. *A terrific performance of wit and zany farce.*

his uniquely malignant Carabosse, with its curious mixture of concentrated sinister rages and sudden flashes of regal dignity. In my opinion (despite having seen some remarkably good performances by other artists), but he has never been equalled, certainly not bettered.

Robert Helpmann as the poet in Apparitions. *A superb vehicle for him in which he made a tremendous impact with his dramatic performance.*

Helpmann's fine renderings of the classics, especially in *Swan Lake* and *Giselle*, were gradually built up becoming famous for many years and unsurpassed dramatically in this country. Apart from Satan in *Job*, his best romantic and dramatic creations for the company were The Master of Tregennis in

Robert Helpmann as Albrecht in Giselle *of whom he made a very likeable boy prince. In his version one felt equally sorry for him and Giselle.*

de Valois' *The Haunted Ballroom*, 1934, The Red King in *Checkmate*, 1937, and, for Ashton, the Poet in *Apparitions*, 1936, followed by the Leader of the Forces of Evil in *Dante Sonata*, 1940. The others were in his own ballets—*Comus*, 1940, *Hamlet*, 1942, *Miracle in the Gorbals*, 1944, and *Adam Zero*, 1946. Helpmann has both acted and danced the role of Hamlet, the ballet being based on the last lingering nerve-distorted brain flickerings of the murdered Hamlet. Only Bobby could act Hamlet alive and dance him dead! The ballet is what is known as 'Dance Drama', a major minor work. *Miracle in the Gorbals*, another 'Dance Drama' was a striking choreographic comment of the times concerned as it was with a famous Glasgow slum. With its curious biblical twist it was a strange, powerful, violent work, both moving and terrifying. It deserved far greater acclaim than it received with its fine appropriate music by Sir Arthur Bliss and equally appropriate sets and costumes by Edward Burra. It was his first ballet *Comus*, based on Milton's masque, in 1941, which showed his potentialities as a choreographer, and in which he gave us the innovation of the spoken word, using parts of *Comus* which he spoke with a soft, musical intonation and a power more personal than vocal, but none the less effective. The production was excellent and much enhanced by Oliver Messel's decor and costumes and Constant Lambert's arrangement of Purcell's music.

In all, Helpmann created over fifteen major roles while with the company, dancing a leading part in more than two score others between 1933 and 1950 when he retired. I have particularly chosen the earliest picture of him in *Giselle*, as I have done with Fonteyn, for they built up a great proportion of their classical reputation, over many years, with their partnership. Helpmann's seniority and 'star quality' undoubtedly helped the young Fonteyn in her fledgling years as a ballerina.

Sir Robert Helpmann is, among his many theatrical activities, a director of the Australian Ballet, but still manages to make periodical guest appearances with the Royal Ballet.

Today Ninette de Valois must be proud that her 'Satanic' protogée 'Bobby Helpmann' is now Sir Robert Helpmann the internationally famous dancer, actor, choreographer, producer, and director of the Australian National Ballet.

A study of Robert Help-mann and Mary Honer as the bride and bridegroom in A Wedding Bouquet *with Margot Fonteyn as Julia.*

Mary Honer as Prometheus' wife in Prometheus. A light comedy role which suited her perfectly.

MARY HONER WAS already a premiere danseuse of some note when she joined the Vic-Wells ballet company in 1935. Its dancers then were rich in talent but comparatively weak in technical accomplishment. She was a pyrotechnical magician of those days, tossing off pirouettes and fouettés as if they were pink gins at a cocktail party. It is therefore no wonder that Frederick Ashton should have cast her as the fouetté-girl in

Les Patineurs. Mary Honer had style and authority but lacked the star quality and dramatic powers so necessary for the complete fulfilment of the greater classics. Many Anglo-Saxon dancers make excellent demi-character dancers, often appearing uneasy in attempting to throw up the more naturally dramatic volcanics of their Latin and Slav sisters. They make splendid Swanildas, finding comedy a more natural form of projecting their images. Probably for these reasons Mary was a first-rate comedienne, making a delectable full-blooded Swanilda, just bouncing through the difficult last act solos and pas de deux. The full length production of this classic in 1940 brought Mary into her own in a big way: one could feel she enjoyed every minute of it, and it is interesting to note that she was the first English ballerina to dance this role in its entirety. Previously only the first two acts had been performed by the company, led first by Lydia Lopokova and then Ninette de Valois in 1933.

In the mid-'thirties, after Markova had left the company, there was nobody capable of doing the full length *Lac des Cygnes* so the young Fonteyn shared the double role, dancing Odette first to the Odile of Ruth French and then to the Odile of Mary Honer. Mary was a tornado of flashing arms, eyes, legs—the lot—ending with a crescendo of fouettés and pirouettes and to maniacal applause. Not subtle maybe; but magnificent.

During the war years, Mary danced in the full length *Casse Noisette*. As usual the technicalities left her completely unmoved and she looked in a pink and white tutu and candy top head-dress, every inch a sugar plum fairy off the top of a birthday or wedding cake.

Mary Honer's balletic prowess was only beaten by her personal courage first shown in the early hours of the morning during the war when she was literally blown up in the Café de Paris. I saw the ghastly mess next day and how she escaped is a mystery. She appeared that same night in *Coppelia*, to everyone's amazement and admiration. She was a real trouper, with the warm, friendly personality usually associated with that type. I remember another occasion when June Brae hurt her foot dancing her solo as the Lilac Fairy in the original production of *The Sleeping Princess* in 1939. Mary took over the role without a bat of the proverbial eyelid, and without any rehearsal. Nobody in the company even thought she knew it. Furthermore, she also danced the roles she created in it of

Mary Honer as 'Papillon' in Carnaval *in which her speed and precision were delightfully invigorating to watch.*

the Violet Fairy, the Diamond Fairy and the Blue Bird. The house went mad with delight at this fantastic feat.

In one ballet Mary Honer surpassed both Markova and Fonteyn, and that was as the Girl in *The Rake's Progress*, she was so typically and plumply Hogarthian, giving a straight rather than stylised dramatic performance. To my way of thinking, this character is always played to advantage by dancers with no trace of Continental blood in their veins. Hogarth is so one hundred per cent English.

In 1937 Honer created one of the best comedy roles of her life as the Bride in Ashton's *A Wedding Bouquet*. It was in this ballet that she had her first big chance of what we would call today a 'camp' take off of the Edwardian days, and Ashton, with his usual sure touch of feeling, created it out of her, arranging his choreography to show off her fine technique and sense of fun inherent in her. She never put a foot, finger or eyeball wrong. She had already shown her feeling for comedy in de Valois' *Prometheus*. Mary also danced the Foolish Virgin in *The Wise Virgins* in 1940—and as such was so charmingly and vacantly foolish! The ballet with its super Renaissance sets and costumes by Rex Whistler, and Constant Lambert's arrangement of Bach's music, was based on the ancient form of Jewish marriage. It was strangely moving and delicate in its religious feeling, but it somehow failed to have the success it deserved. Perhaps it was too gentle for a wartime audience's jangled nerves, which needed tragedy or farce.

The first time I remember seeing Mary Honer dance was the Waltz in *Les Sylphides*, in 1935, just after she had joined the company. With her pleasingly rounded arms and musicality, her rendering of the Waltz was delightful, but it was her Papillon in *Carnaval* that I remember best of all. Her speed, lightness and precision was exciting to watch. The part was created by Nijinska for Diaghilev who chose de Valois to follow her, and de Valois in turn chose Honer. Both were so right.

'Dear old Mary', as she was affectionately called by her colleagues, left the company in 1942 and died in 1965 after a long and tragically painful illness, during which she showed the remarkable courage one would expect of her. A trouper to the end. And I shall always remember her as the company's pyrotechnical pioneer.

13 Alicia Markova

A study of Markova in Pavlova's dance of the 'Dying Swan'.

BEFORE JOINING THE Vic-Wells Ballet company, Alicia Markova had already become a great favourite with the ballet public through her work with Diaghilev as his 'starlet', in her very early teens. After his death, in 1929, she, like the rest of his company, was thrown into the maelstrom of music halls, musicals and revues, until the formation of the Vic-Wells Ballet, the Camargo Society and the smart, popular little Ballet Club run by Marie Rambert at the Mercury Theatre.

In 1933, Markova decided to join the very young Vic-Wells company as a regular member and its prima ballerina, having already made several performances as a guest artist—in fact, she had her first demi-pointe role created for her by Ninette de

Alicia Markova in Giselle. A semi-human being of exquisite delicacy . . . her body seemed entirely detached from this world.

Valois at that time, as Echo in the ballet of *Narcissus and Echo*, with Stanley Judson as her partner. Markova had many far more lucratively tempting offers from other sources but, with her usual foresight, she realised the company needed her and she, it. Thus it was that between the years of 1933 and 1935, when she left to form her own company with Anton Dolin, she reigned supreme rising from the status of prima ballerina to that of a prima ballerina assoluta of the great classics which Ninette de Valois had especially revived for her in their entirety: *Giselle*, *Le Lac des Cygnes* and *Casse Noisette*, all in 1934 a feat of no mean proportions. Neither the full length *Casse* nor *Lac* had been seen before in this country by the general public, so it was a great challenge both to the company and to Markova herself. The effect of such a star upon the company and audiences alike was stupendous and of immense value to their prestige, so we must be eternally grateful for those vital three years of Markova's rapid rise to maturity in her art.

Markova, during this period, danced in many of the lesser classics, namely *Le Spectre de la Rose*, *Les Sylphides* and *Carnaval*. Her musically poetic rendering in *Les Sylphides*, surrounded as she was by moonlight and billowing masses of white tulle, cast her magic spell over all of us, moving as part of the music like trees in the wind. Oddly enough, however, with all her lightness and ethereal qualities, I found her ill-suited to project the warmth of an adolescent young girl's rather sexy dream about a rose, in *Spectre de la Rose*. In *Carnaval,* as Columbine, her performance seemed once again to fall between the warm, humanly adult feminine quality of a Karsavina and the inconsequent charm and gaiety of a youngster. During this period Markova created a few roles outside the classics, including that of The Betrayed Girl in de Valois' *The Rake's Progress*, and Alicia in *The Haunted Ballroom*. Looking back, I realise that I never cared for her in *The Rake*, as she appeared unhappy with the stylised choreography and rather subtle dramatic qualities needed; she appeared too frail for such typically English Hogarthian goings on and looked far more Latin than English. However, in *The Haunted Ballroom*, both the 'feel' of the ballet and its choreography went perfectly with her personality and dancing; she was in her element with her slim lithe body twisting, pirouetting and gliding about like some demented ectoplasm, her transparent, greyish-purple costume alternately clinging to and flying off her body, was both weird and electrifying.

61

Alicia Markova in Les Rendezvous. *Specially created for her by Frederick Ashton. It brought out all Markova's finest qualities.*

For Frederick Ashton she created the charming and slight role of Katie Willows in his *The Lord of Burleigh*, but it was his delectable and scintillating ballet *Les Rendezvous* that really brought out every gift she had with its speedy and stylish pyrotechnicalities. With her ballon amounting to levitation her only difficulty appeared to be how to keep herself out of orbit! The music appeared to flow both with and through her, the greatest thing of all being her fantastic ease of execution. If the music had soared to heaven she would simply have followed it with her little wry smile, and we would have lost our first ballerina assoluta! In *Casse Noisette* the 'grand manner' was tempered by her remarkable grace and fluidity of movement. This was no tinsel Sugar Plum Fairy from a Xmas cake, but an exquisite porcelain figurine, and the famous somewhat acrobatic grand pas de deux in the finale was danced by her with a thistledown lightness and a positively bewildering ease. In *Le Lac des Cygnes*, her Odette gave one the feeling of a being completely mentally detached, allowing the music itself to work through her with all its dramatic, sentimental and lyrical qualities—neither woman nor bird. In the ballroom scene, as the Magician's daughter Odile, Markova was a complete meta-morphis and here she tackled the acting in a completely human way full of personal electricity and magnetism and displaying her remarkably vital virtuosity, even successfully tackling those maddening fouettés, at least on the first performance. In this act, Markova showed the admirable strength and determination of her own character belying the apparent frailty of her body. It was in this ballet that so many people likened her to Pavlova. In fact, the only strong affinity between the two was, in my opinion, their appearance. Anna Pavlova, besides being a great dancer, was a great actress and personally temperamental, to a lamentable degree at times. I well remember the exciting scandal during her season at the Palace Theatre when she soundly slapped her partner's face and walked off the stage—he probably deserved it! If that had been Markova, I feel a cleverly 'arranged' accident would have discreetly, if somewhat more painfully, reminded her partner of her displeasure, with no damage either to performance or reputations. No, I think that Markova and Taglioni were far more alike judging from old criticisms and lithographs, and both became Queens of the Ballet Blanc.

I have seen Markova in all kinds of modern ballets but she decided instinctively, I think, to stick to building up her reputation on the classics and her romantic and ethereal image as a Sylph, Giselle, Sugar Plum Fairy and finally as Princess Aurora in *The Sleeping Beauty*, when she returned after the war to dance again as guest artist for the Royal Ballet. In my opinion this, sadly, came a little too late in her career, for the incredibly long and arduous technical feats demanded of the role. Nevertheless, her star personality, musicality, lightness, artistry and sheer determination overcame most difficulties, making it for these reasons one of the most admirable triumphs of her career.

Markova floated around and above the melting pots of criticism with that quaint little smile and far away look in her large expressive eyes. Herself a wraith, she danced when and how she liked, but with all her apparent intangibility she was intensely practical. She remained as faithful to her public as they were to her, giving them their fill of their beloved romantic ballets of yesterday and today, of which she remained Queen for over thirty years, until her retirement in 1963, her final act of levitation leaving us all with proud and happy memories of the first great English ballerina assoluta.

14 Pamela May

A portrait of Pamela May as Eurydice in Orpheus and Eurydice *Her beauty and serenity, soft fluid plastic movements and aura of gentle tragedy are difficult to forget.*

THE PIONEERING DAYS of the Royal Ballet will always remind me of the remarkably eminent career of Pamela May. After early training with the Royal Academy of Dancing, she became a pupil of Ninette de Valois at the age of fourteen. She made her debut from the corps de ballet in the *Swan Lake* pas de trois in 1934. In her book *Invitation to the Ballet*, de Valois describes the young Doris May (later to become Pamela) as ' . . . beautifully made, a graceful and talented handful . . .!' It was undoubtedly these qualities which helped to make her achievements so successful as Swanilda in *Coppelia,* Violet in Ashton's *Wedding Bouquet,* and, in John Cranko's batty, but brilliantly comic Edwardian romp *Bonne Bouche,* a titilating, scheming, genteel Edwardian matchmaking Ma.

I would describe Pamela May as primarily a demi-character dancer who attained a high position among the ever-growing hierarchy of prima ballerinas. She had the national virtues of graciousness, lyricism and gaiety, plus good looks and immense charm. She was celebrated for her lovely classical line. Torn ligaments, strained tendons and personal wartime adversities were the cause of many breaks in her career. I think all these things tended to affect her strength as she appeared to find it difficult to sustain the full length classics—especially in *Swan Lake,* with its devastatingly difficult third act. Highly dramatic roles were not in Pamela May's repertory and indeed would not have suited her but she was an excellent and subtle comedienne. With a very definite but non-aggressive authority and matching mime she enhanced her characterisations of such roles as the Queen Mother in *Swan Lake,* Bathilde in *Giselle,* the Lilac Fairy, the Fairy Godmother in *Cinderella* (which she created in 1948), and the Queen of the Wilis to which she added just the right amount of malevolence while in her dancing she treated us to some superb jetés and pas de bourrées.

Pamela May reached the peak of her career as a purely classical ballerina when she alternated the role of the Princess Aurora with Margot Fonteyn in 1946, upon the re-opening of the Royal Opera House. She was, in fact, the first purely Anglo-Saxon ballerina to dance the full-length *Sleeping Beauty* —for although Fonteyn's father is English, her mother is of Brazilian descent. Certainly Pamela May must be the only artist who has played both Aurora and the Queen in the same production. (The nearest equivalent I know is that of Carlotta Brianza, who had been the original Aurora in Russia and came back to play Carabosse in Diaghilev's 1921 revival.) Pamela May's *Odette* fairly flowed with her lyricism and purity of line but not from the very depths of so gay and charming a soul could she possibly throw up any form of the sinister to make one believe in Odile who, after all, is a pretty turgid character!

In modern ballets, Pamela created several major as well as minor roles, solos, pas de deux, etc. Among these I think her best were the Red Queen in *Checkmate* (de Valois, 1936), her first creation for the company; *The Prospect Before Us* (de

Valois, 1940); *Orpheus and Eurydice* (de Valois, 1941), and in Ashton's *Horoscope* (1938), *The Wanderer* (1941) and *Symphonic Variations* (1946).

Pamela May as Odette in Le Lac Des Cygnes. *Her dancing of pure classicism was lovely to watch, with its purity of line and lyricism.*

This mixture of modern and classical roles gives some idea of the diversity of her art. Her lovely performance of the Red Queen in *Checkmate* was full of warm, touching sensitivity, imposed upon, yet in sympathy with the stylised choreography, and infusing in to it a remarkable lyricism. Some years later she took on the role of the Black Queen; one missed the sinister sensuality of June Brae's performance, but when one remembered her gentle Red Queen her Black Queen became a terrific *volte face* . . . she was a veritable lioness . . . out for the 'kill' . . . a fine performance of murderous duplicity. As Mlle Théodore, the spoiled dancer in *The Prospect Before Us,* she gave us a full dose of delightful, saucy eighteenth century *coquetterie* and a breezy show of non-Slavonic temperament. Her Eurydice will always be remembered by me for its infinitely poetic qualities; the sheer beauty of the music flowed through her like water in the fountains of Rome, creating an aura of gentle tragedy, difficult to forget and lovely to remember. Her performance in *Symphonic Variations* gave full play to her fine musical timing and classical style. It was in *Horoscope,* as the Moon, that she showed more than a hint of her future career as a classical dancer. Her essays in comedy began with *A Wedding Bouquet* (1937), and continued in *Coppelia* and *Bonne Bouche,* while when the company first restaged *La Boutique Fantasque* (1947) she danced the Can Can dancer with an elegant, infectious, abandoned gaiety. In fact, she was an Anglicised version of her famous predecessors, Karsavina, Lopokova and Danilova—but none the less enjoyable for that.

Widowed during the war, Pamela happily remarried and now has a grown up son and younger daughter. Fortunately she joined the teaching staff of the Royal Ballet School whilst continuing as a most welcome guest artist in the traditional roles where good mime, dignity and stage presence are so important· So, after 38 years, Ninette de Valois' 'beautifully made, graceful and talented handful' has more than fulfilled her early promise, and hands down her fund of experience to future dancers at the Royal Ballet School.

15 Elizabeth Miller

IN 1902 THE pas de trois in *Swan Lake* was danced in Russia by Karsavina, Sedowa and Fokine. The first time the Vic-Wells did it the dancers were Markova, de Valois and Idzikowski. I point this out to show that even in its earliest days this now noted pas de trois was never too lightly treated, so that when Pamela May, Elizabeth Miller and Walter Gore (another ex-Rambert dancer and creator of The Rake in *The Rake's Progress*) took over in 1934, it was one of the first steps up the classical ladder of the future National ballet. It was also Elizabeth Miller's debut as a soloist. In my opinion it couldn't have been a better curtain-raiser for her career, which was cut short by her marriage shortly before the war and her consequent retirement.

Elizabeth Miller joined the company in 1933. She was a typical budding English rose type and her work had an unaffected quality of porcelain delicacy and *joie de vivre* added to which she had considerable technical accomplishment. She was specially selected by Frederick Ashton as his pirouetting Blue Girl in *Les Patineurs*—opposite Mary Honer's fouettées—and I remember on the first night how uproariously the house applauded their concerted brilliance. However, in comparison to Honer, Miller was Scarlatti to the former's Beethoven, which was never so apparent as in her performance of the Betrayed Girl in *The Rake*. According to Arnold Haskell, she 'created much interest by her sympathetic portrayal of the Young Girl, and gave a magnificent performance of Swanilda' (it wasn't until 1940 that the full length version was danced). With both these verdicts I agree, particularly the second. But I found her Young Girl in *The Rake* a trifle too light, lacking the more robust approach of Mary Honer, who danced it later on.

It was in de Valois' *The Gods go a-Begging* that Elizabeth Miller made one of her best impressions; every inch of her few feet was a little Fragonard, porcelain goddess with delicate little features, lightness and poise. In Ashton's *A Wedding Bouquet* she had one of those small but important cameo sketches as Terese, a young, very genteel Edwardian spinster, who wasn't sure of herself or anyone else, afraid to be either shocked by or She created an entirely different role in Ashton's *Horoscope* as the speedy leader of the fiery followers of Leo. Her Song Bird

Elizabeth Miller as Katie Willows in The Lord of Burleigh *an early creation of hers with its agreeably romantic English feeling.*

69

Fairy, which she created for the company's first version of *The Sleeping Princess* in 1939, might well have been tailor-made for her style by the great Petipa himself. I also enjoyed enormously Elizabeth Miller's Columbine in *Carnaval*. It was exhilarating and delightfully playful in all its gay, fresh youthfulness, which really defied highbrow criticism. A performance far apart in feeling from the original production of Diaghilev, with such an exquisite and mature artist as Tamara Karsavina, but this is a ballet which can portray the mood of an era with older and established artists and will be equally, though entirely differently, enjoyed when danced by the younger generation, and I liked it just for that.

The first role I remember Elizabeth Miller created was in a revival of Frederick Ashton's *The Lord of Burleigh* during a season by the company in the early 'thirties. Owing to lack of funds and dancers, particularly with regard to men, there was a pretty wide gap between principals, soloists and corps de ballet (nowadays we have principals, soloists, choryphées and artists) so it would be hard in some cases to place these in terms of today, the gap being far less between each group. However, I think that Elizabeth Miller would certainly rank among the principals of today, despite the generally higher standard of technical abilities required from some dancers, both as executants and artists. But it is the latter virtue, crowned as it was with the exciting, genetic spirit of those days, which was paramount in getting the company to mature in so short a period. Struggling, as they had to, against far more adult and experienced companies visiting London with such famous artists as Tchnernichova, Danilova, Nemtchinova, Woizikowski, Shabelevsky, Eglevsky, Massine—they simply had to produce artists of their own.

How proud and pleased the early members of the company should be with themselves and the great company they helped to build. Elizabeth Miller was one of the many who then worked so hard for so little. Truly those pioneering days were greatly embellished by artists such as Elizabeth Miller, who grew up with the company itself. It was always sad to see them leave, especially when one so often felt that their possible future greatness still lay ahead of them.

16 Ursula Moreton

A study of Ursula Moreton in The Lord of Burleigh *as the weeping Marianne . . . with a madonna like face.*

URSULA MORETON, LIKE Ninette de Valois, was one of Diaghilev's soloists, and my first memory of her was as one of the Porcelain Princesses (with Dorothy Coxon) in the Diaghilev production of *The Sleeping Princess* in 1921. They were two of his 'English' girls, others were Hilda Bewicke, Vera Savina (Vera Clark) and Lydia Sokolova (Hilda Munnings)—the finest artist and character dancer of her day. I believe Diaghilev predicted the future of the English dancer.

When Ninette de Valois laid the foundations of the Vic-Wells Ballet at her dancing academy in 6 Roland Gardens in 1926, Ursula Moreton joined her and was her first principal dancer and teacher, specialising later on in character dancing and mime roles. Of part central European parentage, Ursula Moreton had a Madonna-like face and type of feminine beauty one usually associates with the central European countries. In classical roles she was essentially a demi-character dancer and thoroughly enjoyed the romanticism and lush musicality of the *ballet blanc*. It is, therefore, hardly surprising that she gave her best performances in the Prelude of *Les Sylphides*, 1932, as the Young Girl in *Spectre de la Rose*, 1932, and Chiarina in *Le Carnaval*. It was in this genre that she created the role of the weeping Marianne in Frederick Ashton's *The Lord of Burleigh* in 1932. Her character dancing roles included many Czardas, Polonaises, Mazurkas and the Spanish dance in the original production of *Casse Noisette*—in which she doubled the role of the President's Wife in the prologue. I think her first important role with de Valois was as the Woman in the Camargo Society's production of de Valois' *La Creation du Monde*, before the company itself had been officially recognised. This was followed by many other solos and leading roles mostly in ballets by de Valois, which included *Les Petits Reins*, 1928, *Hommages Aux Belles Viennoise*, 1929, *The Picnic* (The Faun), 1929, *Suite de Danses*, 1930, *Danse Sacrée et Profane*, 1930, *Narcisse and Echo*, 1932, and in *Job*. Certainly in those days work must have been pretty tough despite the intermittent performances and possibly even for that very reason. Later on she created the role of Ursula in *The Haunted Ballroom*.

Ursula Moreton was a born hostess, on and off the stage, and was really often type cast, revelling in such creations as the President's Wife in the prologue of *Casse Noisette*, Madame Noverre in *The Prospect Before Us*, the Countess in *The Gods go a-Begging*, the Queen Mother in *Le Lac des Cygnes*, and the Prince's fiancée in *Giselle*. She also created the roles of the Countess in *The Sleeping Princess* and Cinderella in the last act, a rather dreary little dance into which she managed by some miraculous means, to infuse a great deal of charm and character. However, to my mind, the apex of her creative performances was the Street Dancer in *The Rake's Progress*, a triumph of characterisation and make-up, transforming her handsome, dignified and romantic personality into a debauched Hogarthian strumpet, dancing with complete abandon, sugared with a

ghastly and uncanny form of coy gentility—a vignette worthy of a large canvas. Ursula Moreton remained with the company as dancer, mime and teacher but gave up dancing in 1946 to take up full-time teaching and administrative work, organising and

Ursula Moreton as the dancer in The Rake's Progress. *A triumph of make-up and characterisation.*

co-directing with de Valois The Sadler's Wells Theatre Ballet as an offshoot of the main company, which she later left to become Principal of the Royal Ballet School in 1952. Temperamentally Ursula Moreton can best be described by the title of a famous and lovely book *Quiet Flows the Don*: for instance, when she appeared as the dreaming adolescent girl in *Spectre de la Rose,* I suddenly found myself highly amused by the awful thought that she might not wake up!

When writing about a dancer, teacher, administrator it invariably becomes more difficult to stress the value of their work in a company, in comparison with that of a ballerina, for the pattern is so very complicated and diffuse, the difference between a plain solitaire and cluster diamond ring; the one looks more exciting than the other, but the value is the same. In Ursula Moreton's case one of her greatest values in the company was her perfection of mime, she was not only a 'natural' but also took lessons from Tamara Karsavina to perfect her art, and spent many years in passing it on to other members of the company and to students of the Royal Ballet School. In fact, she was the company's first dancer-mime.

After nearly half a century of working for the organisation Miss Moreton was given an OBE, after which she retired but occasionally took regional auditions for the School until her death in 1973.

17 Sheila McCarthy

Sheila McCarthy. Principal soloist, demi character dancer and teacher as Aunt Marianne in the Prologue of the first English production of Casse Noisette.

SHEILA MCCARTHY WAS amongst Ninette de Valois' earliest pupils in her academy of dancing at Roland Gardens in 1928, becoming one of her first soloists and salaried staff; amongst some papers I found an article by Evelyn Williams, one time secretary to Lilian Baylis, in which she states: 'The Vic was embellished by the presence of Ursula Moreton, Beatrice Appleyard, Joy Newton, Ailne Phillips, Jill Gregory, Freda Bamford, Rosalind Patrick, and Sheila McCarthy. Of these young dancers Rosalind Patrick and Freda Bamford left the company to become actresses, and Jill Gregory became a soloist, teacher and ballet mistress, which position she still holds with the Royal Ballet . . . a difficult, hard working position of vital importance to any company'.

My first memory of Sheila McCarthy was as Procris; a role she took over from Lydia Lopokova in a revival of Ninette de Valois' ballet *Cephalus and Procris,* first produced for the Camargo Society. It was a light colourful eighteenth-century *pastiche* with de Valois as Aurora, Lopokova as Procris, and Stanley Judson as Cephalus. Sheila fully justified the honour by her fresh, gay, youthful charm and vivacity, added to which she had a natural sense of 'theatre'. Old programmes show her performances in one evening alternating between being a choryphée in one ballet, a soloist in another, and a principal in a third, out of the four ballets performed. She found it 'all such fun': perhaps that was due to the fact that they only performed once a fortnight, but it was very hard work, when one considers that on top of this she taught the younger members of the school, gave classes to the drama students and office workers with star-crossed ideas of becoming ballerinas. Those classes possibly formed the nucleus of the ballet 'galleryites' who became so vociferous in their applause, and in their loyalty to the company for so many years. Sheila was also sent all over the country sorting out possible students for the school; during this period she found 'an alarming technically precocious small pupil of eleven, a Miss Groom, who could "do the lot" '; well, Miss Groom joined the school, graduated to the company, was renamed Grey, and as Beryl Grey she was the first English ballerina *assoluta* to be a guest artist of the Bolshoi ballet, and the second one to emerge from the company . . . today she directs the Festival Ballet.

In a similar way Sheila found John Field, whom I remember as a rather lanky, scraggy youth who developed into one of our foremost danseur nobles as Beryl Grey's regular partner in the company and one of its directors in the sixties. However, all this work by no means curtailed Sheila's dancing activities as soloist and principal artist in over twenty-eight ballets until her retirement. She was a demi-character dancer and as such took over several de Valois roles at the Old Vic; I saw her in one at Sadler's Wells as Webster in *A Wedding Bouquet* which suited her sense of characterisation and vitality particularly well, a different, more extrovert performance than that of de Valois.

76

With regard to Sheila McCarthy's work both in classical and modern ballets she was called 'a dancer of character and distinction' by W. P. Manchester, a well respected critic of the time . . . I absolutely agree with her too. I thought that Sheila's creation of 'the woman with the corsets' in *The Rake's Progress* a brilliant representation of a bawdy, sleezy slut, tight as a coote serenading a candle with her corsets . . . maybe only a cameo, but a gem at that . . . so very different from her Papillon in *Carnaval,* and as the gentle, little old lady, Aunt Marianne, in *Casse Noisette.*

So it was that after a varied and successful career of over twenty years with the company Sheila McCarthy left at the beginning of the war . . . some sink into oblivion . . . Sheila swam into marriage. Better than oblivion anyway!

Sheila McCarthy in the role created by her as the girl with the corsets in The Rake's Progress.

Claude Newman as the tailor in The Rake's Progress.

It is only within the last thirty-five years that the male dancer has been accepted at his full value as a man and not a maniac, and is now liable to find himself in the honours list instead of bedlam or worse!

The first record I can find of Claude Newman is in the excellent book on *The Sadler's Wells Ballet* by Mary Clarke in which he arrives as a guest artist by permission of C. B. Cochrane in 1930, when the Company was still more or less a handful of dancers under the direction of Ninette de Valois. He became a permanent member of the Company in 1932 as a soloist and I first remember him in de Valois' ballet of *Douanes* as one of the three Gendarmes. But his first leading part was, in fact, as Mr Bear in a slight ballet called *Uncle Remus* with decor by Hugh Stevenson, music by Gordon Jacob and choreography by Sara Patrick in which one of the six rabbits was the little choryphée Margot Fonteyn. Although not successful with her choreographic debut, Sara Patrick under the name of Sara Payne became an excellent member of the teaching staff and after forty years is still with the Royal Ballet School: a soprano who cannot reach the high C can at the same time be a very fine teacher.

Claude Newman was the company's first male character dancer, mime and teacher. His Dr Coppelius was successfully played on fairly conventional lines: slightly comic: faintly necromantic, a rather doddering old man, more toymaker than magician. Played straight this is a tiresome role and only comes to life when humour and a touch of pathos is integrated, as one

Claude Newman as Drosselmeyer in Casse Noisette *which he played with skill and just the right amount of wizardry.*

79

should feel sorry for the old fool yet laugh at his grandiose ideas of his own mystique and necromancy.

Claude Newman was solely a character dancer and his Buffon solo in *Casse Noisette,* which he created for the company, was our first taste of an English version. He danced it with a fine serve, gaining laurels from the galleryites and press alike.

I use a picture of him as old Drosselmeyer in *Casse Noisette,* a role created by him for the company. His Drosselmeyer was just right in its fussiness and very slight sinister feeling, a charming vernacular period style cameo and followed as it was, by his Buffon in the last act highly impressive. In *The Rake's Progress* he created a delicious study of the tailor with a marvellous make-up and his timing was perfect. He used his needle and thread to purpose as well as effect; even the sudden quick movement of his head as he bit off the thread was musically perfectly timed and somehow always made me chuckle— the note and snap of the thread coincided to a split second. In the Bedlam scene he had another cameo as the mad admiral with a telescope. Such small details in the construction of certain ballets are all-important, particularly in works by de Valois—they must be done right or not at all. The shuffling around in vague backward and sideways movements for a few bars coping with a patched eye and long telescope is far more tricky than a down to earth solo. In *Le Roi Nu* he was again a tailor but this time Chinese, with Ashton and Chappell as his conspirational companions. And how right and funny they were, roguishly fawning, mooching and finicky around their Emperor.

I think Claude Newman's peak performance was undoubtedly as Mr Taylor opposite Helpmann's Mr O'Reilly in de Valois' *The Prospect Before Us* with his mad wig, and fidgety little gestures, he was the perfect foil to the blustering Mr O'Reilly. Teetering, fretting and tottering around in a vacuous elegant and stylish way, he was comically pathetic; a perfect eighteenth century distressed puppet! Later on Newman joined the teaching staff of the Sadler's Wells Ballet School and subsequently appeared with the Sadler's Wells Theatre Ballet. He was the first male member of the company to join the teaching staff of the School, and for a short period he taught for de Valois at the Turkish School. He has also worked in Rome and Brazil, and continued to teach and be an active member of the Royal Academy of Dancing until his death after a long illness in 1973.

19 Joy Newton

Joy Newton as the Queen Mother in Le Lac Des Cygnes. *She had excellent mime, and moved with a pleasing grace and dignity.*

ORIGINALLY A PUPIL of Ninette de Valois, from the mid-'twenties, Joy Newton became one of her first choryphée soloists, character dancers, ballet mistresses and teachers. Under the supervision of de Valois, she was the Founder Director of the Turkish National School of Ballet in 1948, starting with only a handful of small boys and girls. Within a quarter of a century this developed into the Turkish National Ballet of today . . . history repeating itself, but by this time Joy Newton the pupil had become a director.

My first memory of Joy was that of a young, blonde girl with attractive dimples looking as plain as a barn stone one minute and as pretty as a rambler rose the next—quite maddening as it threw one off one's critical balance. She always looked well on the stage, being a good mover and having a potential sense of authority, quite at variance with her dimpled prettiness. This must have caused many a shock to would-be ballet class delinquents!

Between 1931 and 1941 Joy Newton was a choryphée and soloist in no fewer than twenty-three ballets. (I have illustrated here only a few of her versatile representations.) There was

A study of Joy Newton in the ballroom scene from Apparitions.

82

regality and dignity of the Queen Mother in *Swan Lake,* which she created for the company in 1934, the Queen in *The Sleeping Princess* in 1939, the delicacy and charm of a woman of the Edwardian *haute monde* as Beatrice in *The Haunted Ballroom,* with another in *Apparitions,* and as a character dancer in the Czardas in *Coppelia.* In contrast to these, was her salaciously comic vignette of the blowsy and genial street singer in *The Rake's Progress.* I shall never forget her as Love in the prologue of *Checkmate,* playing the chess game of Life and Death, with Frederick Ashton as a suitably grisly figure of Death. She might well have been one of Benvenuto Cellini's most glamorous and immaculately innocent cherubs in her tightly curled gilded wig, her thoughts no doubt on quite a different plane!

When one comes to think of it, Joy Newton had not only an impressive but also a decidedly exciting and hectic career with the company, what with the British Council's well meaning but somewhat misguided effort in sending them on their now legendary visit to Holland on the eve of its invasion, when they were machine-gunned, biffed and buffeted around, giving her the first instalment of wartime theatrical touring. This was swiftly followed by years of London and provincial tours during the Battle of Britain, hardly a rest cure what with their bombs and our shrapnel—the latter often far more tricky than the bombs if one was unlucky enough to be out in the street—it zinged, bounced, hopped and chased around like the famous old Keystone comedy cops, but not quite so funny. Anyway she, and the rest of the company, seemed to get away with it all, often turning that Grand Guignol into a Grand Giggle with their native sense of fun and the ridiculous, also proving Miss Newton wasn't christened Joy for nothing. So all ended well and not a dimple wrinkled. Apart from her stamina and organising ability, Joy was an excellent repetiteur, as her choreographic memory was remarkable and incredibly useful in the revival of old ballets. Choreographers, unlike most people, seem more prone to forget details of their former work. When I last met Joy I thought her far better looking than in her youth, the years having added character and not age to her looks, the dimples still there happily working full time. Not bad after forty years of trials and tribulations devoted to the aims and ambitions of de Valois, the founding and establishing of the English and Turkish National Ballets.

Covered in tulle and ribbons, twisted and twirled around with speed and clockwork precision by her partners. Ailne Phillips created a feeling of mad infectious gaiety in the pas de trois from Les Rendezvous.

WHEN I WAS a young man in the early teens of this century, the ghost of British ballet hovered, glided, flittered and, more often than not, tottered about the music halls and seaside piers of England. Opera was still treating ballet as a rather superfluous art but a tiresome necessity. It wasn't until the early 'twenties that the Royal Carl Rosa Company started taking ballet seriously. The Directors employed Lydia Kyasht, a beautiful and favourite Russian *première danseuse* of the old Empire days, to mount ballets for them. Her young pupil Ailne Phillips became the *première danseuse* until she left to join Ninette de

Valois in her Roland Gardens academy of dancing during the late 'twenties. Like her colleague Joy Newton, she became a member of the Royal Ballet in its pre-natal days.

When I first met her she was a petite girl with fair hair, a round pretty baby face adorned with a lovely infectious smile— at times—and a pair of large and lively eyes. I presume that is why she became known as 'Babs' Phillips. She looked very like pictures of Queen Victoria as a young girl, which I think the illustration here brings out. It shows her in de Valois' original role from the pas de trois in *Les Rendezvous*. There was a distinct similarity about her dancing and that of her last teacher, de Valois. Both were at their happiest in high spirited solos as in *Barabau,* another de Valois creation, but there the likeness ends, for Babs' approach was more direct or English, being full of animation and high spirits, while de Valois was more subtle. It was Gallic wit as opposed to fun. They both had an innate sense of theatre.

When the *Giselle* peasant pas de deux was introduced at Sadler's Wells in 1935 Babs danced it with Harold Turner. I remember being most impressed with her lightness, speed, easy execution and general *joie de vivre* and I felt she enjoyed dancing as much as the audience enjoyed her performance.

I will now quote from *The Bystander,* the weekly periodical I worked for: 'a good technician, strong precise style, a consequential charm and humour of her own . . . suitable to bright impudent roles, as in *Les Rendezvous*'. I cannot think of a more suitable description of her work; furthermore, she had a lyrical quality which she could and did use when necessary. Nevertheless she was far better in demi-character roles, remaining as a principal of the company until the early part of the war, when she took over the management of the school at Sadler's Wells until the general collapse of the theatres, the blastings and bombings compelling the school to close down.

There followed short periods with her old company, The Carl Rosa Opera Ballet, and Mona Inglesby's International Ballet, which she left to rejoin the Sadler's Wells school at its new premises in Baron's Court. Finally she became personal assistant to de Valois upon the re-opening of the Royal Opera House in 1946. Then she became almost everything—working as repetiteur, taking classes, and giving private lessons to the principals. She was the company's most popular teacher for several years. Again like Joy Newton, her pretty, petite appearance belied her activity and quiet determination. Most of the past and present stars of the Royal Ballet owe much to her private lessons, among them Fonteyn, Sibley, Grey, Nerina, Shearer, Elvin, Beriosova and, among the men, MacLeary, Grant, Shaw, Blair and a host of others. Many balletomanes will remember, with a certain nostalgia, seeing, night after night, in 'Madam's' box, two solitary women, de Valois and her shadow Babs Phillips, heads bobbing and nodding like a mild form of Punch and Judy!

During this period de Valois sent Babs out to Ankara to produce *Coppelia* for the Turkish National Ballet. I cannot imagine a more difficult role to play than being a member of a company as well as PA to its Director. In most cases this would lead to split loyalties, but with good sense, humour and, above all, a profound understanding of dancers, plus her dedication both to the company and its director, Babs remained unmoved and immovable! She retired in 1965 but is now back again with the Company as guest teacher.

Ailne Phillips dances a solo in Giselle.

Michael Somes' first star role in Horoscope.

MICHAEL SOMES WON the first male scholarship into the Sadler's Wells Ballet School at the age of seventeen, in 1934. He rapidly graduated into the company and on Boxing Day 1935 he received his first private lesson from Ailne Phillips,

88

herself a principal dancer of the company. Somes was to become our first 'home grown' premier danseur noble, also the first English male dancer to tackle all the classics (Anton Dolin was Irish and Robert Helpmann Australian). For these he had many aptitudes. Musicality (inherited from his father and grandfather, both musicians), a fine physique, extremely handsome and a virile nobility of movement beyond his years. However, in his younger days he appeared to have a far too reserved dramatic approach to his work which did not leave him until after the war.

It appeared to me that it was not until he was twenty-two, when creating the role of the Leader of the Children of Light in *Dante Sonata* that he displayed a latent dramatic awakening. This was just prior to the invasion of Holland when all nerves were strung up and Frederick Ashton, as usual, rose to the occasion with this remarkable and almost hysterical choreographic tour de force. In his dancing Somes developed a

The young Michael Somes in Harlequin in the Street *not yet ready to show much more than his remarkable 'ballon'.*

89

considerable technique and very soon became known for his fine cat-like leaps. I remember watching this extraordinary young man making gigantic leaps across the stage in Ashton's *Les Patineurs*. Again, in *A Wedding Bouquet* as a cheery character called Guy, he bounded about like an agitated stag at mating time. Surprisingly, with all his elevation, he seemed heavy and rather stiff in the famous Bluebird pas de deux—it would appear to need someone 'supple at the waist', a very quick mover and with more ballon than elevation. It suited Stanislas Idzikowski, the perfect type, who first introduced it into the company: an eagle may soar and hover but cannot flutter. However, it was, as I have mentioned, not until after the war that Somes developed into the danseur noble we were to know so well, giving intriguingly, theatrically muted performances of originality and style entirely his own, more romantic than dramatic, sometimes debonair as with his Prince Charming in *Cinderella*, elegant as the Caricaturist in Massine's *Mam'zelle Angot,* rather sultry as Prince Siegfried in *Swan Lake,* and a noble serenity as the Bridegroom in Ashton's *The Wise Virgins,* and so on. His partnering—eventually, after a slow start—was sure, sympathetic, and had a rather fine grandeur about it. He 'presented' his ballerina 'at court', rather than 'showed her off' in the orthodox way. His miming was concise and unfussy, and as Prince Ivan in *The Firebird* I have never seen a finer performance of noble, virile mime. And I have seen a lot of Prince Ivans, including the Russians of the 1930s!

Michael Somes' first star role was created for him by Ashton, as the young man in Constant Lambert's *Horoscope,* in 1937. He danced with Margot Fonteyn, and it proved to be the beginning of a long and famous partnership. The impact he made was considerable, and I quote from a contemporary critic, P. W. Manchester: 'a potential English great dancer'. This prophecy was later to be fulfilled—and for nearly thirty years, through countless modern and classical ballets, he danced with Fonteyn. He created so many roles, great and small, which number more than three score, so many of them invented by that amazing Master, Frederick Ashton. In chronological order—*Horoscope, Harlequin in the Street, Dante Sonata, The Wise Virgins, The Wanderer, Symphonic Variations, Les Sirènes, Scènes de Ballet, Cinderella, Daphnis and Chloe, Tiresias, Homage to the Queen, Rinaldo and Armida, La Péri, A Birthday Offering, Ondine, Marguerite and Armand.*

90

I have seen Michael Somes give superb performances in the role he created as Capulet for MacMillan's *Romeo and Juliet,* in which the eloquence of his mime was fascinating. He spoke with his hands; his dignified, calm but harsh natural dignity and stateliness was finally veiled with a gentle touch of remorse which I found more moving than a more explosive and less subtle performance would have been. Similarly, with his creation of Armand's father in *Marguerite and Armand,* his slow calculated movements and commandingly severe dignity, gradually changing to a show of moving gentleness towards Fonteyn as Marguerite, was touchingly human and lovely to see, like the sudden rays of the sun breaking through an overcast sky. It was the 'muted' performance brought to perfection. I could not help thinking how strange it was and how admirably creditable to see an artist who, for so many years, partnered Fonteyn now acting as her father and, what is more, dominating the scene. All this points to the fact that a male dancer's terpsichorian motto is *Ars longa viva brevis est,* for there is nobody to lift, support or push around the poor male dancer when his physical prowess wanes. Wisely, he becomes actor, teacher, repetiteur, director—or all four like Michael Somes. Watching the performances of such artists one becomes doubly appreciative of their work—pleasure and admiration for the present 'potted up' with nostalgic memories of the past.

After ending his term as a director of the company Michael Somes is still with the organisation as teacher, repetiteur, guest artist, and in full charge of all Sir Frederick Ashton's ballets. I can think of no more suitable person to take charge of the Maestro's choreographic museum.

Harold Turner in
Barabau.

LET'S START WITH a rehearsal taken somewhere, sometime by someone. An exasperated voice is jettisoned from the auditorium. 'Harold, for God's sake stop that pirouetting!' Of course this had little or no effect upon Harold Turner for he was born a top! Thus it was he created the role of The Boy in Blue for Ashton's *Les Patineurs*, which I think was his only major creation for Ashton apart from his earlier one as the Young Bridegroom in *Le Baiser de la Fee*.

He was in his seventh heaven of delight and showed it too. His pleasure communicated itself immediately and at full blast to the vociferous audience as he glided, leapt, spun and generally camped around—entrechats, brisés, pirouettes, grand jetés, following each other with firework brilliance. The effect was terrific, particularly in those days for *Patineurs* was made as long ago as 1938. Ashton saw to it that he did 'the lot'.

Similarly in *Carnaval* as Harlequin his dancing and saucy gaiety bubbled out like water from a burst pipe. In retrospect Turner certainly appealed to me as one of the best Harlequins I had seen. His Bluebird too, which he created for the company in *The Sleeping Princess* in 1939, and danced later in *The Sleeping Beauty*, was delightful to watch. It was a splendidly virile performance of bird-like flutterings and one could well imagine a rather overcrowded nest of fledglings off stage. *Les Rendezvous* was another Ashton ballet which suited him admirably with its technicalities, and touches of exhilarating and frisky geniality.

Prior to the 'thirties it was just not done for tough young Englishmen to become ballet dancers, yet Harold Turner had previously proved himself to be a notable exception to this with the Camargo Society and Marie Rambert's Ballet Club. He had also danced in the commercial theatre, before he joined the Vic-Wells Ballet in 1934. He had a perfect classical technique but was never really successful as a danseur noble. Such people are born, not made. Always wanting to be a danseur noble, he left the company for a time and joined Mona Inglesby's International Ballet where he danced *Swan Lake* and, at the beginning of the war, other ballets. But he later rejoined the Sadler's Wells company. It was then I saw him as Franz in *Coppelia* which I found far more suitable to his personality of breezy heartiness and general amorous gallantry. In addition, there was his triumphantly dazzling solo in the last act. I have heard it said that Harold Turner was not musical, but I do not think this was really so; he was an extremely excitable person and I can well imagine him getting into a spin, physically and mentally, thereby somewhat over-balancing the music and possibly himself as well.

In the early 'twenties and 'thirties it was the flaming ambition of every young male dancer to 'do' the classics which frequently 'did' them instead! Harold, as I have already pointed out, was no exception.

Harold Turner was a fine character and demi-character artist with his technical feats and basic sense of true cockney humour, and during his time with the company, on and off throughout twenty years, he created many memorable roles and danced the lead in many more. Among, I would say, his most important were those in Ashton's *Baiser de la Fee*, 1935, de Valois' *Barabau*, 1937, and as the Red Knight in *Checkmate* in 1937, which was choreographically well tailored for him, being modern in concept with his fine technique being used for dramatic effect rather than for its own sake. He also created two brilliantly opposite roles for de Valois in *The Rake's Progress*, namely The Dancing Master in the first scene and the macabre, violently horrific Man with the Rope in the Bedlam scene. Her choreography seemed to bring out the actor in him. She also gave him a truly comic role in *Barabau*, a slight but wittily amusing contemporary political choral ballet. Later on, Turner took over two other leads in de Valois' ballets, namely Satan in *Job* and The Rake himself, both from Robert Helpmann. In them, he proved himself to be an artist of some considerable dramatic ability already tentatively shown in *Checkmate*. I found his performances both enjoyable and intriguing, especially as The Rake. In comparison to his predecessor, Harold attacked and danced the role with magnificent gusto whilst Helpmann intellectually out-manoeuvred him, dramatically. A Donald Wolfit and John Gielgud of the ballet world. I think this applied to Turner's Satan in *Job*, too; his was an evil and outstandingly virtuoso performance, and excitingly satisfactory.

Towards the end of his career Harold Turner made ballet history by being the first Englishman to dance Massine's famous roles of the Can Can in *La Boutique Fantasque* and the Miller in *Le Tricorne*, both in 1947. I had always admired Harold's character work but was amazed by his performances in both these ballets. I quote a contemporary critic with whom I thoroughly agree: 'his rich sense of comedy and excellent character dancing well fit him to follow Massine'.

Harold retired to teach at the Royal Ballet School in 1950, occasionally appearing as guest artist—such as in 1954, when he was the Burgomaster in *Coppelia*

In 1962 it was decided to revive another Massine ballet following the success of the others, namely *The Good-humoured Ladies*, and Harold Turner was to play the part of the old Marquis. From the start controversy raged around this revival and at the end of a rehearsal Harold collapsed and died. This shocking and sudden end of such a popular, gay, warmhearted artist cast a deep depression and sadness upon the company and all those who knew him, both as an artist and personally. The human top had spun to a halt. I feel sure Harold would have wished it that way.

94

Harold Turner as the red knight in Checkmate.

Epilogue
Constant Lambert

Constant Lambert joined the Vic-Wells Ballet in 1931 as its conductor and musical adviser, remaining with the Company (except for a short period of illness) to become one of the directors in 1942 until his death in 1953.

His own compositions, namely Rio Grande, Horoscope and Tiresias, were much influenced by the Jazz era with its predominance of saxophones and percussion, but they always retained a purely classical basis. The initial terrifying experiences of the war – the invasion of Holland – followed by everlasting bombstrewn wartime tours, incessantly playing the piano for performances without an orchestra; advising, composing, and arranging scores from Chabrier to Beethoven, plus eternal dreary black-out train journeys, undoubtedly helped considerably towards his gradual tragic deterioration and death. I always thought it sad that Constant's strenuous work for the Company never gave him time to develop as a composer by putting its importance before his own creative career, and was also undoubtedly the reason why the Company only had three of his works in its repertoire.

He was a most delightful and satisfactory person to be with. A true *bon viveur*, and one could never be bored listening to him whether on ballet, opera, theatre, books or anything. He had a delightfully unvicious wit, but he could, and did, upon suitable occasions make it devastatingly 'dry'. My old friend Arnold Haskell once described him as the 'Lully' of English Ballet, and except for the fact that Lully was a *danseur* as well as musician and that poor Constant walked with a stick, the analogy is excellent!

Constant's work for the Company was beyond valuation; with his good taste, sound judgment, and commonsense, he was entirely responsible for the Company's high mucial standards, and the Royal Ballet, which the Company is called to-day, should for ever be grateful and proud of the pioneering work done by its first musical director. He understood dancers, loved, lived and worked for ballet . . . the 'evening star' of the Royal Ballet's musical history.

Constant Lambert. Composer, conductor, author.